Whose What?

Whose What?

Aaron's Beard to Zorn's Lemma

Dorothy Rose Blumberg

HOLT, RINEHART AND WINSTON

NEW YORK   CHICAGO   SAN FRANCISCO

To my father,
who found especial delight
in Bach, Emerson, and Mark Twain.

Author's Note

When the project of collecting *Whose What?* first got under way, it seemed little more than an enjoyable exercise. I had no idea how far the search would lead or into what diverse fields. But as time went on, curiosity took over and interest grew, and so did the number of items that complied with the simple ground rules: the "who" must be a person, real or legendary; the "what" could be, but did not have to be, something other than what was literally meant by it. Thus *cat's cradle* and *baker's dozen* were barred; while *Aristotle's lantern* and *Newton's fits* are not at all what one might expect.

Suggestions came from many quarters. Friends were helpful in all sorts of ways, calling me at odd hours or sending little notes to say "Did you think of—?" To all of them, my sincere thanks, and very special thanks indeed to my husband, whose idea it was in the first place!

As to sources, these include biographies, histories and manuals; old diaries and newspapers; biographical, medical, mathematical, classical, and other specialized dictionaries and encyclopedias. Footnotes would have been a nuisance, but supporting references are tucked into the text where useful.

The collection is obviously far from exhaustive. As proposed entries piled up, the problem of selection arose. "Laws," "diseases" and "theorems" exist by the score, and choices had to be arbitrary. In general, the determining factor throughout was either that the item was little known but interesting or that some unexpected or unusual information could be offered on a familiar subject. Readers will undoubtedly have their own ideas as to what might have been included and will come up with many more suggestions that meet the guiding rule.

—D. R. B.

Brief description
Aaron's Beard to Zorn's Lemma
BY DOROTHY ROSE BLUMBERG

About the Author

DOROTHY ROSE BLUMBERG has been a student of word usage from the time that she passed an Anglo-Saxon course with flying colors until the present day. She is the author of *Florence Kelley, The Making of a Social Pioneer,* and is now at work on another biography.

Mrs. Blumberg lives in New York City with her husband and has been beset by friends and fellow researchers for over a year with suggestions of strange expressions that ought to be explained.

Aaron's Beard

(Great St.-John's-wort, *which see*). A perennial herb of the saxifrage family (Latin *saxa,* a stone, and *frangere,* to break) that thrives in rocky crevices and mountain areas; marked by especially prominent tufts of hairlike stamens which were used, probably in the same way that cobwebs once were, to stanch bleeding.

There is a reference to the healing virtues of this herb in *Complaynt of Scotland,* a work published in 1548 or 1549 and attributed to the Scottish patriots Robert Wedderburn, James (or John) Inglis, and David Lindsay. Chapter 6 tells of someone wandering in a meadow full of plants and herbs most convenient for medicine, who remarks, "I sau ane herb callit barba aaron, quhilk vas gude remeid for emoroyades of the fundament" ("I saw an herb called barba aaron which was a good remedy for hemorrhoids of the rectum").

Aaron's Breastplate

A vestment worn by Aaron, the first high priest of Israel, and made, according to directions given by God to Moses, of "gold, blue, and purple and scarlet stuff and fine twined linen." It measured a span (about 9 inches) in length and breadth and was set with 12 stones in 4 rows: sardius, topaz, and carbuncle; emerald, sapphire, and diamond; jacinth, agate, and amethyst; beryl, onyx, and jasper; one stone for each of the sons of Jacob, engraved with their respective names, and all held in place with a filigree of gold (*see* Exodus 28:15–21).

Aaron's Rod

The name applied to a number of tall, flowering plants, such as goldenrod and mullein. In archaeology, it designates a rod with a single serpent twined around it, perhaps harking back to the biblical story in which Aaron cast down his rod before Pharaoh and the rod became a serpent. The Oxford English Dictionary says the figure is sometimes, but erroneously, called the caduceus of Mercury. The true caduceus has two serpents and its rod often bears a pair of wings, in addition.

Abraham's Bosom

An area on the border of Hell, known as *sinus Abrahae* (cave of Abraham) or *limbus Patrum* (limbus of the Fathers), where, according to medieval theology, the Old Testament saints were supposed to have dwelt until Christ descended there and freed them.

The biblical reference to Abraham's bosom occurs in the story of Dives and Lazarus. As told in Luke 16:22–23, "The poor man [Lazarus] died and was carried by the angels to Abraham's bosom. The rich man also died and was buried; and in Hades, being in torment, he lifted up his eyes and saw Abraham far off and Lazarus in his bosom."

The first theological use of the term *limbus,* which means *border,* is ascribed to the philosopher St. Thomas Aquinas (1225–1274) in his *Summa Theologica.* Much earlier, the church Fathers had perceived only two destinations for the soul: heaven for the saved or baptised; hell for the sinful damned. Later disputations brought up the question of what should be the fate of those not good enough for eternal bliss, yet not deserving eternal punishment. The concept then grew of an intermediate place, a *limbus Patrum,* for those who had led exemplary lives but died unbaptised, and a *limbus infantum* or *puerorum* for infants who died before the rites could be carried out, as well as for those to whom baptism could have no meaning—idiots, for example.

In the *Divine Comedy* of Dante Alighieri (1265–1321), *limbus* becomes *limbo,* the first circle of hell. Here the shades of great men, such as Homer, Hector, Caesar, Socrates and Plato, Hippocrates and Averroes, are encountered by Dante and Virgil, his guide. Virgil explains:

> ". . . Ere thou pass
> Farther, I would thou know, that these of sin
> Were blameless; and if aught they merited,
> It profits not, since baptism was not theirs,
> The portal to thy faith. If they before
> The Gospel lived, they served not God aright;
> And among such am I. For these defects,
> And for no other evil, we are lost;
> Only so far afflicted, that we live
> Desiring without hope." Sore grief assail'd
> My heart at hearing this, for well I knew
> Suspended in that Limbo many a soul
> Of mighty worth.

Today, limbo is still used to denote a state of being cut off from normal relationships, of being nowhere.

Achilles' Heel

Any fatal weakness of character. The term is taken from the Greek myth in which Achilles, invulnerable in the rest of his body, is killed during the last days of the Trojan War when struck in the heel by an arrow from the bow of Paris.

The youngest of seven sons born to the sea goddess Thetis and the human Peleus, Achilles, like his brothers, inherited his father's mortality. To spare her children the common destiny of death, the silver-footed Thetis, as Homer calls her, placed them in a bed of flames one by one as they were born, so that when their mortal parts had been consumed, the immortal elements might rise to Olympus and eternal life.

When Achilles was a few days old she began the ritual

for him, anointing him with ambrosia by day and laying him in the fire at night. This time Peleus came upon her in the midst of the ceremony and cried out in horror. Thetis dropped the baby and fled away to the sea forever. In spite of the interruption, Achilles was rendered invulnerable except for one ankle bone which had been scorched but not wholly burned.

Another version of the story has it that the rites were carried out not with fire but with water. Thetis is said to have taken the infant to the banks of the Styx, the River of the Dead that flows around Hades, and carefully lowered him into the dark waves. However, she had gripped one heel so tightly that it remained untouched by the magic waters.

As Achilles grew to manhood he passed unscathed through a thousand risks and perils, including the long years of the Trojan War. Then came the encounter with Paris. Some say the god Apollo guided the arrow to the one vulnerable spot, others that Apollo assumed the guise of Paris and loosed the deadly weapon himself. Whether inflicted by man or god, the wound was fatal and Achilles perished.

Adam's Ale

Jocular reference to water, that being the only beverage served in the Garden of Eden. The Scots call it *Adam's wine*.

Adam's Apple

(Adam's morsel). The thyroid cartilage of the larynx, seen at the front of the throat and generally more noticeable in men than in women. It is an old wives' tale that when Adam took a bite of the apple offered by Eve, the morsel stuck in his throat and so became an eternal reminder of man's first sin.

Adam's Needle

(Needle-and-thread). A species of yucca (*Yucca filamentosa*), member of the lily family, flourishing in the sandy soil of the Southern and Southwestern United States, Mexico, and Central America; also known as *bear grass*.

The yucca seems to be something of an all-purpose plant. Its species vary from low bushes to trees 30 or 40 feet high with stiff, sword-shaped, pointed leaves and are much culti- vated for ornament. Some bear fragrant creamy white flowers, others an edible purple fruit. From the stalks and foliage a coarse fiber is obtained, which is twisted into rope. The slender leaves of bear grass are woven into chair seats.

The connection with Adam may stem from Genesis 3:7, which tells how, after having eaten of the fruit of the tree of knowledge, Adam and Eve "sewed fig leaves together and made themselves aprons," presumably using the fibers and sharp spines of a plant resembling the yucca.

Adam's Peak

A cone-shaped mountain in southern Ceylon, one of the highest (7,360 feet) of that island's many mountains; so-called for an indentation resembling a giant footprint in the rocky surface of the summit.

There are at least three legends to account for the "foot- print." According to Mohammedan lore, it was made by Adam, who was forced to stand on one foot as a 1,000-year penance after having been driven from the Garden of Eden. Hindus say it is a relic of the god Siva, the Destroyer. The Buddhists (their faith became Ceylon's state religion about

the 3rd century B.C.) claim that it is the mark of Gautama
Buddha's foot, set there when he visited Ceylon for the
third and last time to preach to the people.

Today the sacred spot is still the goal of regular pilgrimages during the ceremonial months of March and
April. Worshipers climb the steep road, stopping occasionally along the way at resting places built almost a thousand
years ago by King Vikramāditya. At Kelaniya they visit the
dāgaba, a relic shrine in the shape of a hemisphere topped
by a spire, erected at the place where Buddha once stayed
and move on to Samantakūta at the summit, where, in the
area guarded and tended by Buddhist monks, they do hom-
age to the great teacher.

Adam's Rib

A colloquial term for a woman, from the biblical account in Genesis 2:21–22 which states that Eve was fashioned out of a rib taken from Adam while he was in a deep
sleep.

Addison's Disease

Characterized by bronzing (pigmentation) of the skin
caused by malfunction of the adrenal glands due to lesions
on the cortex, often resulting from tuberculosis. The disease
is accompanied by low blood pressure, weakness, excessive
perspiration, and progressive anemia. It was first described
by Thomas Addison (1793–1860) of Guy's Hospital, London, and was usually fatal before the recent discovery of
the cortisones, with which a certain amount of relief can
be established and maintained.

Apollo's Chariot

The sun, represented in Greek mythology as a golden vehicle drawn by four fiery steeds, in which Apollo, as the god of light, drives across the sky each day.

Apollo, "Lord of the Silver Bow," was the son of Zeus and Leto and twin of Artemis, the virgin huntress. Exceptionally handsome, he was the god of music, poetry and dance, of healing and prophecy, the protector of herds and flocks, and the patron of youth and youthful sports. In time, he came to be worshiped also as the god of light, spiritual as well as physical, and in this role as Phoebus Apollo he took over many of the attributes of an older sun god, Helius.

As portrayed by the earliest Greeks, Helius was the son of the Titans, Hyperion and Thia, and brother to Eos and Selene. He, too, is represented as young and handsome, crowned with rays, and driving the famous chariot. After his day's journey, Helius is said to fall asleep in a golden boat or a golden cup, in which he is borne back along the northern edge of the earth to his eastern rising point. Each day before he starts out, his sister Eos, "the rosy-fingered dawn," drives to Olympus in her own golden car drawn by two white horses to tell the gods that her brother is on his way.

Helius had a son, Phaëthon, by the nymph Clymene. One day the boy, boasting to his companions of his divine parentage, was challenged to prove it. He went to Helius, who assured the boy that they were indeed father and son and offered to grant him any gift as proof. Phaëthon asked to drive the sun chariot for a day. Helius was aghast, for he knew the inexperienced boy would never be able to control the horses; but he had given his word. The result was disaster. Ignorant of the path he should take, Phaëthon could not guide the animals properly and the monsters of the sky—Scorpio, Crab, and Serpent—frightened him. Lacking the accustomed firm hand on the reins, the horses bolted and ran wild, first soaring so high that the earth shivered and the North Star glowed with heat, then plunging down so close to earth that the grass caught fire, the rivers boiled, and men living near the equator had their skins permanently blackened. Zeus, to save Creation, hurled a thunderbolt and struck Phaëthon dead. Like a burning star, his body fell into the river Eridanus, whose nymphs bore it to shore and built a tomb for it. When Phaëthon's mother and sisters came to the riverbank to mourn, they wept so pitifully that the gods turned them into poplars, which still stand at the river's edge weeping tears of amber.

Archimedes' Principle

The law stating that when a solid is immersed in a fluid, "the solid will, when weighed in the fluid, be lighter than its weight in air by the weight of the fluid displaced." It was discovered by one of the greatest of ancient mathematicians, Archimedes of Syracuse (c. 287–212 B.C.) in the course of investigating whether a crown made for the tyrant Hiero II was pure gold or had been adulterated with silver.

The principle is Proposition 7 in Archimedes' treatise *On Floating Bodies*. The story of its discovery is well known but bears retelling. Hiero II of Syracuse in Sicily, reputed a kinsman of Archimedes, had vowed a golden crown to the gods. He gave a goldsmith a certain weight of gold to make the crown. When it was delivered, it showed the proper weight; but Hiero suspected that some of the gold had been replaced with an equal weight of silver and called upon Archimedes to investigate the matter.

While mulling over the problem in the baths one day, Archimedes noted that the lower he sank in the tub the more water ran over the rim. It then occurred to him that the amount (or weight) of the water displaced bore some relation to the amount (or weight) of the body that was displacing it; and further, that a denser body, being smaller for a given weight, would displace less of the fluid. Gold is denser than silver; therefore a given weight of it would bulk less than the same weight of silver. It is said that Archimedes, jubilant at having found the clue to Hiero's problem, sprang out of the bath and ran down the street shouting, "Eureka! I have found it!"

Later, putting his reasoning to the test, he took a lump of gold and one of silver, each equal in weight to the crown. In turn he sank crown, gold and silver in a vessel of water filled to the brim, and observed the amount of overflow. His guess was confirmed. The crown displaced more water than did the solid gold, less than the solid silver. Archimedes thus proved that the goldsmith had in fact substituted some silver for gold.

So great, indeed, had his fame become that, when Syracuse fell to the Romans, the conqueror Marcellus gave orders that Archimedes was to be especially protected. It is one of the ironies that during the occupation of the city, a soldier came upon him absorbed in outlining a geometrical figure in the sand. Not recognizing the old man, and perhaps provoked by Archimedes' supposed remark, "Do not destroy my diagrams," the soldier ran him through.

Ariadne's Thread

A magic ball of golden thread used by Theseus as a guide into and out of the labyrinth, where he slew the flesh-eating Minotaur.

In revenge for the death of his son Androgeus at the hands of the Athenians, King Minos of Crete demanded that every nine years they send him a tribute of seven youths and seven maidens to be devoured by the Minotaur. This monster, with the body of a man and the head of a bull, had been born to the king's wife Pasiphaë.

Years earlier, according to Greek myth, Minos, before assuming the throne of Crete, had sacrificed to Poseidon and asked for a sign from the god confirming his right to rule. Thereupon a magnificent white bull rose dripping from the sea and trotted onto the shore; it had been sent by Poseidon to be sacrificed in his honor. But Minos, struck with the bull's beauty, substituted another, and added the sacred animal to his own herd. Angered at this affront, Poseidon caused Queen Pasiphaë to fall prey to an unholy passion for the white bull, which she was able to gratify by enclosing herself in the lifelike replica of a cow cunningly constructed by the master smith Daedalus. The Minotaur was the result.

The Athenians had paid tribute twice, the unfortunate young people being selected by lot and carried to Crete in a ship with mourning-black sails. The third time, one of the band was Theseus, reputed a son of Poseidon and adopted by King Aegeus of Athens to be his heir. Some say Theseus' lot was drawn, others that King Minos came to select the victims and chose him first; most commonly, he is said to have endeared himself to his people by volunteering to go.

When the ship arrived in Crete, Minos came down to meet it, was attracted by one of the maidens, and would have taken her for his household. Theseus boldly intervened, saying that as a son of Poseidon he would protect the virgins in his care. Minos mocked him for his claim to kinship with the immortals and threw a heavy gold ring into the water, saying that as a son of the sea god he should be able to retrieve it. Theseus dived into the waves and with the help of the Nereids brought up the ring.

The king's daughter, Ariadne, who was watching, fell in love with Theseus. Late one night she came to him in secret

and offered to help him if he would take her back to Athens
with him. In addition to a sword she gave him an enchanted
ball of thread that, as he unwound it, would lead him to
the center of the Labyrinth. Perhaps she held the end of
the thread herself, or Theseus may have tied it to the door
lintel. Paying out the magic yarn, he made his way in darkness through many twists and turns to the heart of the
maze, killed the monster, which he offered as a sacrifice to
Poseidon, and returned to Ariadne. With the rest of the
Athenians they then set sail, having first damaged the hulls
of the Cretan ships to delay pursuit.

The Cretans give a different account of their amorous
queen. There was no labyrinth, they say; the Athenians
were merely kept in dungeons until sacrificed or given out
as prizes at the funeral games for Androgeus. At these
games a consistent winner was one of the king's generals,
Taurus, a powerful athlete, arrogantly boastful of his prow-
ess. When Theseus arrived in the black-rigged ship, he asked
permission to take part in the games. The Cretans had long
resented Taurus, and Minos himself had suspected an active
liaison between Pasiphaë and the general, to whom one of
the children bore a striking resemblance. His request
granted, Theseus wrestled Taurus to three falls and sent
him off stripped and humiliated. So pleased was Minos that
he set the Athenians free and gave Ariadne to Theseus in
marriage.

On the way to Athens the ship put in at the island of
Naxos for rest and refreshment. Ariadne slept longer than
the others and awoke to find the ship's sail vanishing over
the horizon. Some say Dionysus had come to Theseus in a
dream and commanded him to leave her. The weeping
Ariadne called upon Dionysus for vengeance. He appeared,
fell in love with her, carried her off, and married her. His
wedding gift was a glorious gem-studded crown fashioned
by Hephaestus; after Ariadne died, it was set among the

northern constellations, where it is known as the *Corona Borealis* or Northern Crown.

Aristotle's Lantern

The name applied to the bony mouth structure of sea urchins (Echinoderma), first described by the Greek philosopher Aristotle (384–322 B.C.) in his great work on natural history, the *Historia Animalium*.

Echinoderm means prickle skinned, an appropriate term for the unlovely sea creature that looks like an oversized chestnut burr. Legless, living mouth downward on the ocean floor, the sea urchin depends for food on whatever is swept its way by the lowest currents. It belongs to the same family as the starfish, and, when dissected, shows the same five-branched configuration. An outer skin covers a thin, globular shell divided into five sections. The prickles are attached to the shell by a ball-and-socket joint, and are used primarily for protection, sometimes for locomotion, occasionally for urging bits of food toward the mouth.

> The urchin has five hollow teeth inside [observed Aristotle], and in the middle of these teeth a fleshy substance serving the office of a tongue. . . . The mouth-apparatus of the urchin is continuous from one end to the other, but to outward appearance it is not so, but looks like a horn lantern with the panes of horn left out.

Aristotle came upon the little creature during a two-year sojourn on the island of Lesbos. The philosopher, then some forty years old, had left Plato's Academy in Athens and was engaged in a series of investigations into "these beings that are the work of nature," the first time anyone had systematically gone about sorting, taking apart (hardly dissecting, as we know it), identifying, and classifying. With the large number of facts thus assembled, he reasoned, it would then be possible to search out common attributes, to

generalize, to discover the universals embodied in the par-
ticulars.

There is scarcely a field of classical learning to which
Aristotle did not make a unique contribution. Logic and
metaphysics, ethics and aesthetics, physics, astronomy, and
the nature of dreams, he studied them all, and his writings
continually reflect the enthusiasm and delight with which
he examined his world. "In all nature there is something of
the marvelous," he wrote in *De Partibus Animalium*. ". . .
we should study every kind of animal without hesitation,
knowing that in all of them there is something natural and
beautiful." Even the legless sea urchin.

Dr. Arnold's Rugby

Rugby is both a boys' school in Warwickshire, England, and a game, forerunner of modern football, which
originated there. The school is celebrated in Thomas
Hughes's *Tom Brown's Schooldays,* a story that takes place
during the 14-year headmastership at Rugby of Dr.
Thomas Arnold from 1828 to 1842.

Avogadro's Hypothesis

Under the same conditions of temperature and pressure, equal volumes of gases contain the same number of
molecules (Latin *molecula,* little mass). This hypothesis
was advanced in 1811 by the Italian physicist Count Ama-
deo Avogadro de Quarenga (1776–1856).

Avogadro's Number

(Avogadro's constant). 6.0248×10^{23},* the number
of molecules in 1 gram molecule (or mole) of any substance. A gram molecule is that amount of substance whose

* 602,480,000,000,000,000,000,000

weight in grams is numerically equal to the molecular weight of the substance, *e.g.,* a gram molecule of oxygen, which has a molecular weight of 32, weighs 32 grams.

Babbage's Analytical Engine

A mechanical calculator, forerunner of the digital computer, it was invented in 1834 by the English mathematician Charles Babbage (1792–1871).

The initial idea for an all-purpose, automatic calculating machine was due to Charles Babbage. There had already been a number of attempts to speed up the process of calculation. One of the earliest efforts, in 1617, was known as *Napier's bones* (*which see*), a non-mechanical device which multiplied only.

The first *mechanization* of an arithmetical process came in 1642, when Blaise Pascal (1623–1662) built for his father a small machine that could add and subtract and was worked by turning a series of geared wheels. In 1671, Gottfried Wilhelm Leibniz (1646–1716) invented a machine that multiplied and divided by successive additions and subtractions. Other devices, more or less obscure, followed during the next 150 years, but all were limited by the need to reset the machine for each step of calculation.

The first real breakthrough came with Babbage's plan for *automating* the entire calculation process. As early as 1812 he had begun to work out a design for a "difference engine," a machine that would use finite differences to compute mathematical functions. The analytical engine, the principle for which he discovered in 1834, was the direct ancestor of such present-day digital computers as ENIAC, UNIVAC, and NORC.

Although Babbage spent the rest of his life on his two inventions, neither was ever finished. Work on the difference engine was dropped in 1842 when the government withdrew its support. On the other hand, the analytical engine, although theoretically sound, was too advanced in concept for the technology of the day. Not until the 20th century brought the age of precision tools and electronics, could full advantage be taken of Babbage's brilliant thought.

Bacon's Rebellion

An uprising of Virginia colonists in 1676, led by Nathaniel Bacon (1647–1676) against the governor, Sir William Berkeley, in protest at the latter's repressive political policies and his refusal to mount a defense against raids by the Indians.

At first glance Nathaniel Bacon would seem the most unlikely sort of person to have led a rebellion. From a noble English family (related to Sir Francis Bacon), educated at Cambridge, and married to the daughter of a nobleman, Bacon had come to Virginia in 1674. Here he acquired several estates, and in recognition of his talents was soon made a member of the Governor's Council, "for gentlemen of your quality," Berkeley had told him, "come rarely into the country, and therefore when they do come [are] used by me with all respect."

That respect did not last long. Under Berkeley, grievances in the colony had been piling up: taxes that discriminated against the poorer planters; severely restricted suffrage; no elections for 9 years to a House of Burgesses controlled by the Governor to his advantage and that of his cronies. The Indian raids were the last straw. Actually, the attacks were in retaliation for English incursions into treaty-protected territory. Berkeley was profiting from a lucrative fur trade with the tribes and stood to lose it if the colonists took up arms. This is exactly what they did. Organizing their own army of defense, they turned for leadership to Bacon, whose sympathies were openly with the small planter and the disenfranchised.

At the head of 300 angry men, Bacon went to the Governor and asked to be commissioned. The request was curtly denied. Bacon led his company into battle anyway and inflicted a heavy defeat on the raiders. In reprisal he was declared a rebel.

By now, however, the whole colony was aroused, and Berkeley was compelled to call new elections for the Assembly. Bacon, despite the pronouncement against him, was elected a delegate, and on June 5, 1676, went to Jamestown to take his seat. He was forthwith arrested, then as abruptly pardoned and promised the commission. After waiting a reasonable length of time, he gathered his men again and marched on the courthouse to force the issue. Berkeley, seeing the building surrounded, dashed to the door and flung it open, then bared his chest and shouted, "Here, shoot me—fore God, fair mark!" What Bacon wanted, however, was not the governor's life but a commission, which was finally granted.

Now a major general, Bacon set off with an army of 1,000 men on a campaign against the Indians. But Berkeley once more declared him a rebel, and ordered some 1,200 troops from neighboring Gloucester County against him. The men refused to fight Bacon, who, returning from a victorious engagement at Bloody Run, laid siege to Jamestown on September 13. Three days later the town was abandoned, and on September 19 it was burned to the ground.

Several more weeks of heavy fighting followed, during which the weather turned wet and treacherous. Weakened by exhaustion, Bacon came down with malaria and died on October 1. The rebellion collapsed, and Berkeley exacted so bloody a revenge that the next year he was called back to England and a lieutenant governor was sent to replace him.

"The old fool has put to death more people in that naked

country," Charles II commented, "than I did here for the murder of my father."

Balaam's Ass

The animal who reproached her master, the Gentile prophet Balaam, when he beat her unjustly.

After wandering 40 years in the wilderness, the Children of Israel were camped on the plains of Moab. They had already defeated two Palestinian kings; Balak, King of Moab, feared he would be the third. He therefore ordered the seer Balaam to go and curse the Israelites that they might be overcome in battle.

Balaam at first demurred, having been warned by the Lord in a dream that he must not carry out the King's command. But after an even more peremptory message brought by Balak's couriers, Balaam saddled his ass and set out with the King's men although he knew he would be able to speak only such words as God put into his mouth.

On the way an angel, invisible to the little company, took his stand in the middle of the road. Only the ass saw the angel and so turned aside into a field, whereupon Balaam struck her a great blow with his stick. The ass returned to the road, but a bit farther on, the angel once more bestrode the path and the ass moved aside and was again beaten. A third time the angel stood before them, so that they could not pass at all. The ass folded her legs and lay down, nor would she move though Balaam rained blows upon her.

Suddenly the animal raised her head, opened her mouth, and spoke. "What have I done to thee, that thou hast struck me three times?" "Why," said Balaam, "thou has made sport of me. And if my stick had been a sword I would have slain thee." "But have I not served thee faithfully to this very day? Have I ever failed thee?" And Balaam had to answer, No.

At that moment the prophet's eyes were opened, and he

too saw the angel standing with drawn sword. Fearful and contrite, Balaam offered to abandon his mission, but he was told to proceed. When he finally climbed a hill above Moab and looked down upon the hosts of Israel, not curses but a blessing issued from his lips and a prophecy of victory for the sons of Jacob.

The Book of Numbers, which contains the story of Balaam, is part of the Hexateuch (the Five Books of Moses plus Joshua). These books are a combination of two versions, one written about the 10th or 9th century B.C., the other somewhat later. They are differentiated by the fact that the earlier one uses the term *Jahweh* to name the Deity, and hence is referred to as the J version; the other, the E version, uses *Elohim*. While there is a difference on a number of details in the Balaam story, the versions agree on one point of particular interest: that it is possible for a man to be a true prophet and yet not be a Hebrew.

Talking animals are quite common throughout folklore. In the Bible, however, the only other instance is the serpent in the Garden of Eden.

Bekhterev's Nystagmus

Nystagmus is the involuntary back-and-forth movement of the eyes, alternately fast in one direction and slow in the other, such as occurs when one sits in a rapidly spinning chair. The Russian physiologist V. M. Bekhterev (1857–1927) discovered that a temporary nystagmus can be induced in a dog by removal of the labyrinth of one ear, the slow eye movement then being toward the good ear; a much more prolonged nystagmus will occur when the labyrinth of the other ear is removed, with the directions of the slow and rapid eye movements being reversed.

Belshazzar's Feast

The royal banquet given by the Babylonian king, Belshazzar, son of Nebuchadnezzar, at which, after wine had been served in the sacred gold and silver vessels taken from the temple in Jerusalem, a hand appeared and wrote on the wall: "Mene, mene, tekel, upharsin" (literally: "he counted, counted, weighed, and they divided"). The story is told in Daniel 5.

Daniel was called before King Belshazzar and promised rich gifts if he could interpret the strange words. *"Mene,"* said the prophet, "means that God has numbered the days of your kingdom and brought it to an end; *Tekel,* you have been weighed in the balance and found wanting; *Parsin,* your kingdom is divided and given to the Medes and Persians." Grateful that the message, though ominous, had been made clear, the King bestowed the promised gifts upon Daniel. That night, the story continues, Belshazzar was slain and his kingdom taken over by Darius the Mede.

According to biblical scholars Belshazzar was not the son of Nebuchadnezzar (the King who, having forsaken godly ways, became as a beast in the field and ate grass like an ox), but of Nabonidus, the last King of Babylon. Belshazzar himself was never King. His name, as inscribed on ancient tablets, is Bel-sarra-uzur, meaning "May Bel protect the King"; and as the first-born he held the offices of Prince Regent and Commander of the Babylonian army. He was also a man of some property, who let houses and loaned money.

Babylon was not conquered by Darius but by Cyrus, who invaded the land in 539 B.C., the 17th year of the reign of King Nabonidus. The King fled to safety. Belshazzar, however, may have been killed in the skirmishing that accompanied the generally peaceful surrender of the city.

Belzoni's Tomb

The sepulchre of Seti I (son of Rameses I, founder of the 19th dynasty), located in the Valley of the Tombs of the Kings in Western Thebes and so-called because it was first opened in 1817 by the Italian archaeologist Giovanni Battista Belzoni (1778–1823) and his wife.

Giovanni Belzoni was the son of a barber in Padua, and was educated to become a monk. He soon found that this was not his vocation, married, and in 1803 migrated with his wife to London. For a while the two were desperately poor, but their fortunes improved when they were befriended by the antiquarian Henry Salt (1780–1827), through whose intervention they joined the circus known as Astley's Royal Amphitheatre. Their act was built on feats of strength, with Belzoni appearing sometimes as Hercules, sometimes as Apollo. Giovanni was quite tall–6 feet, 7 inches–and his wife was a fair match.

In 1815 the couple went to Egypt with a hydraulic machine Belzoni had invented to be used in raising the waters of the Nile. That same year Salt was appointed consul general there, and he sent Belzoni to Thebes for the delicate task of removing the great head of Rameses II (the "Young Memnon") and shipping it to the British Museum. Other archaeological explorations followed–at Edfu, at Abu-Simbel (Salt paid the expenses incurred in the excavations there), and at Karnak. Belzoni's greatest find was the magnificent burial place of Seti I, carved out of living rock and containing, among other treasures, the elaborate alabaster sarcophagus of the monarch.

During the next two years, the Belzonis extended their investigations. At Giza they were the first to explore the pyramids thoroughly, uncovering in the course of their labors the hidden entrance to the second pyramid, that of Chephren, brother of Cheops (4th dynasty). Then in 1819 they returned to England, taking with them a set of drawings of the Theban tombs, the Seti sarcophagus (now in the Soane Museum in London), and a number of other valuable artifacts. The following year Belzoni published a *Narrative* describing their excursions and observations.

Buoyed up by these successes, the couple set off again in 1823, this time for West Africa, intending to go to Timbuktu. They got as far as Benin in southern Nigeria, but shortly thereafter Belzoni came down with a fatal case of dysentery and died on December 3.

Bluebeard's Wives

Seven beautiful women, all but the last of whom were put to death by their indigo-bearded husband for having entered a forbidden room; the lucky lady, Fatima, was rescued in the nick of time by her brothers.

The Bluebeard legend has a number of versions, the most famous and familiar of which is found in a collection of tales by the French author Charles Perrault (1628–1703). The stories were published about 1697 under the title *Histoires ou contes du temps passé avec des moralités* (*Stories or Tales of the Past with Moral Lessons*); and the flyleaf bears the further inscription *Contes de ma mère l'Oye* (*Tales of My Mother the Goose*).

Perrault's 7 Mother Goose tales should not be confused with the later collection of nursery and kindergarten Mother Goose rhymes, which first appeared in print around 1760 and are of British ancestry. Perrault's tales were written in prose, although he cast his *moralités* in verse. His "Bluebeard" has two such moral lessons, as if to fortify his warning against the dangers of giving way to curiosity and trespassing.

With one or another variation the essential ingredients of the Bluebeard story have been found in many parts of the Old World. A Middle-European version records eleven victims, with the twelfth saved by a gooseherd (or a page), whom she rewards by becoming his wife. The Grimms tell of three sisters, the third of whom releases the other two, all then being saved by their brother.

The French tale comes from the northwest coastal province of Brittany, and attempts have been made to give it historical foundation. Andrew Lang (1844–1912), the Scottish journalist, historian, and poet who edited Perrault's *Contes* in 1888, writes in his introduction that Bluebeard (or Barbe-Bleu) had been variously identified as a mythical 6th-century Breton prince named Cormorus or Comorre, and as a 15th-century marshal of France, the Baron Gilles de Rais or de Retz. However, Lang goes on to say, the significant elements making up the traditional story are found in countries where Comorre and de Retz were never known.

Boyle's Law

The law states that at a constant temperature the volume of a gas is inversely proportional to the pressure. It was formulated in 1662 by the Irish scientist Robert Boyle (1627–1691), one of the founders of modern chemistry.

Boyle's law was discovered through experiments on the properties of air. Knowing that air can expand and be compressed, Boyle compared it to a heap of many small, springlike bodies. These bodies become more densely packed near the bottom of a given volume because of the weight of the ones above, and so they constantly seek to expand. An account of his investigations, published in 1660, drew criticism from several sources, and it was in the context of his answers that Boyle propounded his law on the relation between volume and pressure.

Educated at Eton, which he entered at 8, and by travels abroad with a French tutor, Boyle began his scientific career at the early age of 17. He was one of the first members of the Invisible College, a group of scientists and philosophers formed about 1645 and generally credited with being the forerunner of the Royal Society of London (chartered in 1662). Elected president of the Royal Society some years later, he declined to serve, since the office required taking an oath, which was against his principles.

Although Boyle believed in the possibility of alchemy, which included the transmutation of base metals into gold, his experiments in chemistry led him to challenge one of its chief notions, the *tria prima* or three principles. These, as described by the alchemist Paracelsus (1493–1541), were *mercury,* which was thought to impart metallic properties to substances; *sulphur,* responsible for inflammability; and *salt,* which insured resistance to heat. One or another of the three was said to be a component of every known substance. Boyle refuted this claim by producing a counterexample. In *The Sceptical Chymist* (1661), he reported that it was impossible to extract any of the three from gold, and therefore they could not be *the* elements or principles, since not all bodies contained them. He then put forward his own concept of an element, ". . . certain Primitive and Simple, or perfectly unmingled bodies; which not being made of any other bodies, or of one another, are the Ingredients of which all those call'd perfectly mixt Bodies are immediately compounded, and into which they are ultimately resolved." By "perfectly mixt" he meant chemical compounds as distinguished from mechanical mixtures.

It was this definition of an element, together with Boyle's further notion that matter was ultimately composed of "corpuscles" differing in size and shape, that helped move 17th-century science along the path away from alchemy and that much closer to the modern world of physics and chemistry.

Boyle's 30 Acres

An area in Jersey City (at the time owned jointly by John P. Boyle, a paper-box manufacturer, and the Public Service Company), part of which was leased by fight-promoter Tex Rickard to be the site of the Dempsey-Carpentier world's heavyweight championship bout on July 2, 1921.

The 30 acres were really 34, and the plot of ground was known at the time as Montgomery Circle. Earlier it had been Montgomery Park, home of the Jersey City baseball team of the old Eastern League; in 1921 it was still largely vacant land. The proposal to locate the fight there met with a number of objections, but after lengthy negotiations that involved Governor Edwards, Mayor Hague, and the Jersey City Chamber of Commerce, Tex Rickard closed the deal to lease 6½ acres at a "nominal price," and work on the arena was begun early in May.

The publicity build-up had the Rickard flair. Georges Carpentier had fought briefly in World War I, while Jack Dempsey had worked in the shipyards. Rickard cast Dempsey as the villain, calling him a draft dodger, while Carpentier was hailed as the amiable, likeable young soldier. The Frenchman's press photographs were all blond smiles, the American's were dark, heavy featured, and scowling.

Odds on Dempsey were 3 to 1 with no takers. The 8-sided bowl that held the boxing ring was jammed with 90,000 fans, 80,000 of them paying customers who had contributed to the record gate of 1,600,000 dollars. The first live radio report of a prizefight was broadcast with Graham McNamee as announcer, while telephone lines direct to Times Square carried a blow-by-blow account to the crowd, estimated at more than 4,000.

Then in the fourth round it was over; the pride of France was laid low, with a broken thumb to boot. America was jubilant. The stately *New York Times* devoted almost its entire front page and six or seven pages following to one or another aspect of that world-shaking event. They did manage, however, to find room in column one for the story headlined, "Harding Ends War. Signs Peace Decree."

Broca's Area

(Convolution of Broca). A portion of the left frontal region of the brain, demarcated in 1861 by the French surgeon and physical anthropologist Paul Broca (1824–1880) and held by him to control the articulation of speech. This discovery was once taken to confirm the hypothesis that control of various bodily functions is strictly localized to specific regions of the brain, an hypothesis no longer accepted in this extreme form.

Buridan's Ass

A hypothetical beast that stood between two bales of hay, unable to decide which to eat until it starved to death. This quandary is often cited to illustrate the problem posed by the French philosopher and scientist Jean Buridan (*c.* 1295–1356), which was: Given two equally desirable alternatives, how is a choice to be made?

The problem, as put by Buridan, originally involved not an ass but a dog starving between two equally tempting dishes of food and is found in his commentary on a passage from Aristotle's *De Caelo* (*On the Heavens*). In this passage, the ancient Greek philosopher is criticizing an earlier theory that the earth maintains its position because it is equidistant from all other celestial bodies and therefore has no "impulse" to move in any direction. Rejecting that view, Aristotle draws an analogy with "the man who though exceedingly hungry and thirsty, and both equally, yet being equidistant from food and drink, is therefore bound to stay where he is."

Buridan encountered what is now called the problem of reasoned choice in the absence of preference while inquiring into the relationship between will and reason. He argued that man must will (or do) that which reason tells him is the greater good, though he is free to delay his choice until reason has had sufficient time to examine whatever may be at hand to influence his decision. But when all the alternatives are equally attractive and reason has nothing on which to base a decision, a paralysis of will results, and no action or choice can be taken or made.

Modern philosophy introduces the notion of randomness. The task then is to demonstrate the appropriateness of random choice in the case of (1) symmetry of knowledge and (2) symmetry of preference. Given a choice between A and B, there are, under 1, three possibilities: to find some reason based on knowledge for selecting A over B; to find some reason based on knowledge for selecting B over A; to select A or B *impartially* or randomly. Since A and B are equally known (or unknown), reason based on knowledge is excluded, and the third possibility is the only one. Under 2 there are also three possibilities: to find some reason for preferring A over B; to find some reason for preferring B over A; to ignore preference and select at random. Again, if A and B are equally to be preferred, there are no guideposts for reason, and random choice is all that is left.

How Buridan's dog became Buridan's ass remains a mystery, since the writings on will and reason never mention the latter animal. It has been conjectured (by Sir William Hamilton) that Buridan may have referred to the creature while lecturing on determinism, and this was picked up by opponents to deride the doctrine. Or it may simply be that Buridan used the term *ass* so often in propositions illustrating his *Sophisms,* (as, for instance, "A horse is not an ass,") that a metamorphosis eventually took place.

Caesar's Wife

Pompeia, second of Caesar's three wives. Caesar, while a Roman magistrate, divorced Pompeia, sternly remarking, "Caesar's wife must be above suspicion."

When Pompeia was married to Gaius Julius Caesar in 67 B.C., he had just returned from a year's service in Spain and was deeply involved in Roman politics. Ambitious for both prestige and power, he embarked on a number of activities intended to win the affections of the plebs (including the revival of trial by popular assembly) and quickly rose in public esteem. In 63 B.C. he was elected to the highly coveted and powerful position of *pontifex maximus,* with duties which embraced jurisdiction over the ceremonies of expiation, consecration and marriage, regulation of the calendar, administration of the laws of worship and adoption, and the like. The following year he was rewarded with another office of great distinction, that of civil judge or magistrate (*praetor*), entitled to wear the purple-edged toga and be attended by two lictors. It was at this point that scandal broke.

One of the most sacred Roman observances was that honoring the mysteries of the Bona Dea, the "good goddess," deity of fertility of both the earth and women. Her rites were celebrated twice a year—on May 1, marking the dedication of her temple on the Aventine Hill, and in December, at the home of one of the high magistrates. The ceremonies were attended only by women, all males, including the house servants, being strictly barred. The shrine of the goddess was decked with a profusion of plants and flowers and libations of wine were offered.

In December, 62 B.C. the home of the magistrate Julius Caesar was granted the honor of welcoming the worshipers of Bona Dea. Dressed in their ceremonial robes, the Roman women, including Pompeia, had just begun their ritual when it was discovered that a man was in their midst, draped and hooded. His disguise snatched away, the intruder stood revealed as young Publius Clodius, patrician by birth, wealthy, eloquent, and of notoriously loose morals. Outraged, the women fell upon him with their fists and drove him out into the street; but the damage was done, the mysteries had been profaned by his presence.

What relationship, if any, there actually was between Clodius and Pompeia has never been proved. Plutarch, in his life of Caesar, says the young man was in love with her and she "had no aversion to him." On the other hand, E. S. Beesley, writing in the *Fortnightly Review* (May 15–August 1, 1866) of the well-known feud between Cicero and Clodius, vehemently defends the latter, pointing out that Cicero nowhere includes this particular charge in his indictment of Clodius, that in all probability Pompeia was older by a substantial number of years, and that—Plutarch says this too—Caesar himself brought no accusation against the youth. Nevertheless, the desecration occurring in his own house with his wife present was a shame upon Caesar, and shortly afterward he had the marriage dissolved.

Castle's Intrinsic Factor

Hypothesized in 1929 by the British biochemist, W. B. Castle, as a factor which must be present in the gastric juices if the body is to be able to absorb the anemia-preventive vitamin B_{12}. Later (1954) the factor was identified by other workers as a small protein molecule, apparently missing in patients suffering from pernicious anemia.

Cleopatra's Needles

Two Egyptian obelisks, originally set up at Heliopolis about 1500 B.C., one of which now stands on the Thames Embankment in London, the other behind the south wing of the Metropolitan Museum of Art in New York City.

We don't know who first playfully dubbed these monoliths "Cleopatra's Needles"; actually they have nothing in common with the royal ruler other than their Egyptian origin. Obelisks, from the Greek *obelos,* a spit or pointed pillar, are known to have existed as early as the 4th dynasty, about 3100 B.C. They generally stood in pairs at the entrance to a temple and were dedicated to the sun in all its phases, from rising to setting (the pyramids symbolized the sun after it had set). The sides of the shafts were often covered with hieroglyphs, and the peaked crown was sheathed in polished brass or gold to reflect the rays of the sun god Ra.

Heliopolis, at the apex of the Nile delta, was the center of the ancient sun cult. There, the sacred columns were brought to their greatest size and perfection during the 18th-dynasty reign of Thutmosis III (1595–1565 B.C.). Among these columns were the two Cleopatra's Needles. In 14 B.C. they were taken from the temple at Heliopolis by the Roman emperor Gaius Octavian Augustus, nephew of Julius Caesar, and sent to adorn the Caesareum at Alexandria. They stayed until 1877, when the Khedive of Egypt, Ismail Pasha, "presented" one to Great Britain and the other to the United States. The Pasha's generosity roused something of a storm among his people, and it was not until two years later that the way was cleared for transfer of the gift.

William K. Vanderbilt, persuaded by Chauncey Depew and Judge Ashbel Green, put up 75,000 dollars to bring over the obelisk, with the understanding that he and the New York City Parks Department would decide where to place it. Once Egyptian workmen had pried the Needle out of its ancient bed, it had to be eased on shipboard with special rigging and a special cradle. After a stormy ocean voyage the vessel finally reached Staten Island and steamed slowly up the Hudson to dock at 96th Street. Then came the problem of moving across town. Lashed to a caisson-like vehicle, the 60 feet of solid stone was drawn cautiously through the city's streets, traveling only at night when traffic was at a minimum. It took three months to go from the Hudson River to the museum site at 79th Street and Fifth Avenue.

On October 9, 1880, in a Masonic ceremony, the cornerstone of the pedestal was laid. After the stone was set, small amounts of grain (for plenty), wine (for joy), and oil (for peace) were poured on it by the Grand Master, who closed the ritual with: "I declare this stone to be well and truly laid." Setting up the monument itself took several months more; and on Washington's Birthday, 1881, the obelisk was formally turned over to the city in a ceremony held in the large hall of the Museum.

The hieroglyphs, deciphered and translated, turned out to be a record of three rulers. The central columns on all four sides tell of the glories of Thutmosis III, calling him "The Horus, Strong-Bull-Beloved-of-Ra, the king of Upper and Lower Egypt," and so forth. On the margins flanking the center inscriptions, Rameses II (1388–1322 B.C.) recorded his own exploits. Then Osarkon I (c. 960 B.C.) had his name in cartouche form chiseled into the edges of each side.

The New York committee buried a number of articles in a strong box embedded at the base: medals of presidential likenesses to 1880, a copy each of the *Congressional Directory* and the *Army Register* for 1880, a facsimile of the Declaration of Independence, a compendium of the ninth census, a model of the propeller of Admiral Farragut's flagship, a *Webster's Unabridged Dictionary,* and the complete works of Shakespeare.

Cleopatra's War Trumpet

A mocking reference to the Egyptian sistrum with which Cleopatra armed a number of the men sent into the fatal battle of Actium. The sistrum was a religious rattle used by priests during the worship of Isis to indicate various parts of the ritual. It consisted of a more-or-less circular hoop of metal, with crossbars carrying small metal bells loosely passed through holes in the hoop, the whole attached to a handle. The sistrum was sometimes shaken, sometimes struck with a rod, and the sound was believed effective against evil spirits.

Colter's Hell

A volcanic region of boiling, sulphurous springs and fantastic rock formations in the vicinity of what is now Yellowstone National Park. It was discovered in 1807 by the Kentuckian John Colter, a former member of the Lewis and Clark expedition.

A beaver trapper by trade, John Colter had been a member of the expedition commissioned by President Jefferson to explore the northwest reaches of his Louisiana Purchase. Starting off in 1803, the explorers reached the Pacific after some 30 months of charting prairies, mountains, lakes, and rivers. For the return trip the men separated, Captain Meriwether Lewis taking one group along the Marias River in what is now northern Montana, while

Lieutenant William Clark, with Colter in his band, moved south to follow the "Roche jaune" or "Yellow-rock" river.

Somewhere along the way Colter asked for and received permission to leave the company and struck off on his own to resume trapping operations. By 1807, he had established a trading post at the mouth of the Bighorn. As he continued westward, to where the Shoshone branched off from the Bighorn, he came upon a landscape straight out of the *Inferno*. Not for nothing was the Shoshone known as the Stinking River and Stinkingwater.

So fearsome and incredible was Colter's account of his find that most listeners back home refused to believe him. But in 1870 an expedition organized by the territory of Montana explored the whole area thoroughly; and two years later, after a United States government survey, Congress voted that 3,000 square miles, mostly in territorial Wyoming and with a narrow strip each in the territories of Idaho and Montana, be set aside in perpetuity as a national park.

There is no Colter landmark within the boundaries of Yellowstone National Park. The actual spot of Colter's Hell, appropriately enough, lies outside of that scenic paradise.

Coogan's Bluff

A high cliff on the west bank of the Harlem River, at the site of the old Polo Grounds (now a public housing development), part of the property belonging to furniture dealer and real-estate man James J. Coogan (1846–1915), once would-be candidate for Mayor of New York on the United Labor Party ticket, later (1899–1901) Democratic Borough President of Manhattan.

Born in New York, James Coogan graduated from New York University's law school, and then became an install-

ment furniture dealer on the East Side. When his wife's
father died and she inherited the large tract of land that
included the bluff, Coogan added real estate to his furniture
business.

He had larger ambitions. In the spring of 1886, after
almost the entire Board of Aldermen had been indicted for
taking bribes, a group of indignant citizens met to appoint
a Committee of One Hundred to select suitable candidates
for the November mayoralty elections. Coogan, who was
one of those appointed, seems to have expected the committee to back him for mayor. Instead, the committee passed
a resolution that none of its members could be a candidate
and selected Andrew H. Green as the nominee.

The labor unions were also looking for a candidate, and
the name most frequently mentioned by the United Labor
Party was that of Henry George. But somewhere along the
line Coogan received, or thought he had received, a bid to
be Labor's candidate. Two days before Labor's September
nominating convention, the Committee of One Hundred
found Andrew Green ineligible and moved to reconsider
its no-member-a-candidate resolution so that Coogan might
be nominated. The apparent choice of two organizations,
Coogan resigned from the committee and opted for the
Labor Party.

What led Coogan to suppose that he was Labor's
choice is hard to fathom. Henry George's nomination had
been assured by the collection of more than 30,000 supporting signatures during the summer. On September 23
Coogan and a noisy group of followers turned up at Claren-
don Hall, but their efforts to stampede the Labor Party
Meeting were drowned in applause when Henry George was
nominated by John Casserly of the Carpenters, and sec-
onded by Frank Ferrell, Negro leader of the Knights of
Labor. Making one more try, Coogan's lieutenants insisted
on further nominations. Someone in the crowd then

shouted, "I move we nominate James J. Coogan on the installment plan," which was followed by "I second the nomination on the installment plan." The results of the balloting were decisive. The 409 delegates gave Henry George 360 votes. There were 18 complimentary votes from the horse-car drivers for President Thorn of the Second-Avenue Surface Railway, and Coogan got 31.

In the November election Henry George ran second with 68,000 votes while the Tammany candidate, Abram S. Hewitt, won with 90,000 votes.

In 1897, the offices of the Borough Presidents were created, and two years later James Coogan was elected for a two-year term in Manhattan.

Coxey's Army

A group of unemployed men organized by Jacob S. Coxey in the spring of 1894 to march on Washington, D.C., and ask the government for jobs.

In the spring of 1893 the Philadelphia & Reading Railroad went into bankruptcy, setting off a chain of business failures that plunged the United States into the worst depression then on record. Within a year more than 2½ million men, 17 to 19 percent of the labor force, were tramping city streets looking for work.

City governments made some feeble gestures, but anything beyond "self-help" ran into the objection that state or Federal aid would set a dangerous precedent, undermine the worker's self-reliance, and destroy his moral fiber.

Jacob S. Coxey, a self-made Massillon (Ohio) businessman of considerable means, proposed putting the unemployed to work building roads, which needed doing anyway. He persuaded several Congressmen to introduce a bill providing funds for road construction and renovation. Congress, however, proved reluctant to pass the measure, whereupon Coxey announced that he would take "a petition with boots on" to Washington to press for action.

Easter Sunday, 1894, was the day set for the army of unemployed to leave Massillon, unarmed and on foot. Coxey, now dubbed "General," had predicted 100,000 marchers, but only about 100 showed up, accompanied by half again as many newspapermen. The straggling but cheerful column swung down through the principal industrial towns of Pennsylvania, whose inhabitants poured out each night to hear Coxey and others tell why they were there. On May Day, more than a month after the start, some 500 pairs of boots resounded along Washington's Pennsylvania Avenue.

The Capitol itself was the objective. Coxey had a permit to march, but the law prohibited any sort of demonstration on Capitol grounds. Senator William V. Allen of Nebraska, genuinely worried about the growing misery of the jobless, had advised his fellow Senators to appoint a committee to meet with Coxey and hear him out. Instead, the marchers found their entrance to the grounds barred by a solid phalanx of police, with additional police reserves and even Federal troops deployed throughout the city.

Coxey, Carl Browne (whose beliefs in a "Commonweal of Christ" gave the marchers their nickname of Commonwealers), and a man named Christopher Columbus Jones moved forward to talk to the police, who refused to let them through. The three men dodged past the guards and made for the Capitol, however. Halted at the steps and again denied permission to speak, Coxey handed out a prepared statement of protest to reporters. The police closed in, arrested Browne and Jones, and took them off to jail; but for some reason they released Coxey to join his waiting wife and child. A large crowd of watchers, who had cheered the marchers at their first appearance, cheered again. The sudden shout startled the edgy police, who began raining blows with their nightsticks. In the stampede that followed some 50 persons were bloodied or trampled.

The unprovoked attack drew sharp criticism, and the House was called upon to investigate the affair. On May 21st, Coxey, Browne, and Jones were sentenced to 20 days and fined 5 dollars—all three for carrying banners on Capitol grounds, and Coxey and Browne for walking on the grass.

Coxey served his sentence along with Browne and Jones, and was released on June 10th. He was nominated for Congress from the 18th Ohio district, but lost the race, and lost again the following year as the Populist candidate for governor. In 1931 he was elected Mayor of Massillon for a two-year term. He died in 1951 at the age of 97.

Cú Chulainn's Fort

An earthwork or motte at what is now Dundalk on the east coast of Ireland. Associated with the Irish folk hero, Cú Chulainn, who is said to have lived there after his marriage, it is constructed with sloping sides, flattened on top, surrounded by a ditch, and crowned with a wooden fence or palisade, such as the invading Normans built wherever they settled.

According to legend Cú Chulainn hailed from the eastern kingdom of Ultonia, a part of old Ulster, and originally bore the name Setanta. He began his exploits at six, when he killed the watchdog of the smith Culann and, standing watch himself, was given the name Cú Chulainn, "the Hound of Culann." Later, as a youth, he studied the art of war under Scathach, a famed woman warrior.

An ancient Ultonian law required each warrior to have a shield with a distinctive design. When Cú Chulainn ordered his shield from the armorer, the man confessed that all of his ideas had been used up and he could think of no new device. The hero stormed and threatened, but to no avail, and he finally stalked off in a rage. Shortly thereafter a stranger came to the workshop and asked the armorer why he was sad. The armorer explained his difficulty and was told to clear the floor and sprinkle it with ashes "to the depth of a man's foot." Then, with a forked stick called *luath-rindi* or "ash-graver," the visitor drew a design for the shield that was utterly different from any seen in the kingdom, after which he disappeared and was never seen again.

Thus armed, Cú Chulainn went on to perform mighty deeds of valor. At one time, when Ulster was invaded by forces from the kingdom of Connacht, he is said to have held off the advancing hordes singlehanded. He was finally slain, while still a young man, by a warrior from the kingdom of Munster.

Custer's Last Stand

The Battle of the Little Big Horn (1876) between the troops of Lieutenant Colonel George Armstrong Custer (1839–1876) and a force of Sioux Indians under Sitting Bull, in which Custer and all his men were killed.

After serving with distinction in the Civil War, where he rose to the rank of major general, George Custer applied for a leave of absence to serve as commander of cavalry under Benito Juárez, then fighting to liberate Mexico from the Emperor Maximilian. Permission was denied and Custer was made a lieutenant colonel of the 7th Cavalry Division and set to fighting Indians. He won what has been called a smashing victory against the Cheyennes in the campaign of 1867–1868 (actually a massacre of the innocent village of Washita in Oklahoma, during which Chief Black Kettle lost his life); this was followed by a peace treaty. The next five years were quiet ones for Custer, in the course of which he wrote a book of memoirs, *My Life on the Plains.*

By the treaty of 1868 the Sioux had been allotted a reservation in the Black Hills of the western Dakotas, in return for which they agreed not to bother surveyors and workmen for the Union Pacific railroad then moving toward the coast through Nebraska and Wyoming. But in 1873 another group of railway surveyors, this time for the Northern Pacific, began to push across the Dakota plains trespassing on Sioux territory. The Indians retaliated with raiding parties, and the following year Custer and his cavalry were called out to protect the railroaders.

That summer news of a gold strike in the Black Hills was picked up by a number of Midwestern newspapers, who demanded that the Government take over the territory forthwith. More temperate heads urged caution, and the following spring the tribal chiefs were invited to Washington, D.C., to discuss the sale of their land. Nothing was settled at the time. In the fall the commissioners went out to the reservation where they offered two alternatives: a yearly payment of 400,000 dollars for the mining rights or outright purchase of the Black Hills area for 6 million dollars. Both alternatives were rejected.

The next winter (1875–1876) the Army suddenly decided to call all the Indians back to the agencies. But the weather was bad, travel was difficult, and many simply did not show up. The entire Sioux tribe were declared belligerents, and a full-scale military campaign was mounted against them.

The outcome was really never in doubt. In June, 1876, Custer's regiment, part of the troops under General Alfred Terry, was making its way through southern Montana. Advance scouts brought back word of a Sioux encampment near the Little Big Horn River. Judging his company sufficient, Custer ordered an attack. He was badly mistaken. The Indian forces were far larger than he had anticipated.

By the time the battle was over, Custer and his 264 men had been wiped out.

For the Indians it was eventually a losing battle. Perhaps the best comment on their hopeless situation had been made two years earlier by *The New York Times* on the occasion of Custer's first entry into the Black Hills, "We have always observed that when white men want a reservation, it is at once discovered that the Indians have no honest use for it."

d'Alembert's Dream

(*Le Rêve de d'Alembert*). A sequence of three "conversations," set down in the fall of 1769 by the French philosopher and Encyclopedist Denis Diderot (1713–1784), which inquire into the nature of matter and the meaning of life and are at the same time a witty and devastating attack on conventional morality, metaphysics, and belief in the supernatural.

One of the most versatile philosophers of the French Enlightenment, Diderot is perhaps best known as editor-in-chief of the *Encyclopédie*. His bold approach delighted many and offended many others. Twice the official censor suspended and then grudgingly reinstated the publishing license, and for what were suspected of being atheistic ideas hidden in such earlier writings as *Letter on the Blind* (*Lettre sur les Aveugles*), Diderot served a short jail term at Vincennes in 1749.

By the time he came to write *d'Alembert's Dream,* Diderot had mastered large areas of mathematics, chemistry, biology, anatomy, medicine, and science in general. He was therefore well equipped to develop his own philosophy of science, a nondogmatic materialism. The *Dream* itself, written in sprightly and quite uninhibited language, was of course a fantasy, but the problems it discussed had been subjects of Diderot's speculations for many years.

The first "Conversation" is between himself and d'Alembert. Diderot has been describing the universe in materialistic, atheistic terms. D'Alembert, although a skeptic, hesitates to eliminate God. Diderot undertakes to prove that a Divine Providence is unnecessary, since, to one degree or another, all matter possesses "sensitivity," and whatever reactions take place can be explained as entirely physical and mechanical. As for d'Alembert's uncertainties, Diderot comforts him with the thought that "our real opinion is not the one from which we have never wavered, but the one to which we have most regularly returned," and sends him off to bed.

The second "Conversation" is titled *D'Alembert's Dream* and involves first Dr. Bordeu and Mademoiselle de L'Espinasse and later d'Alembert, who has been asleep behind a curtain. Mademoiselle de L'Espinasse tells the Doctor that d'Alembert has been talking in his sleep, continuing his argument with Diderot, and she has taken notes. The dialogue then develops three themes: first, animal reproduction, man included, is mechanical and is subject to occasional breakdowns and mutations; second, the structure of the body may be compared to a spider and its web, the spider being the nerve center in the brain and the web the nervous system with threads running to all parts of the body, damage to any of the threads resulting in various aberrations both mental and physical; and, finally, psychological and moral behavior can thus be adequately accounted for in purely physiological terms.

The third dialogue, a *Sequel to the Conversation,* is between the lady and the Doctor. Here Diderot draws several startlingly modern conclusions, among them that crossbreeding and other eugenic experiments are not only possible but might be desirable; and that physical acts, provided they do not harm society, another person, or the individuals engaging in them, are not the concern of morality.

Such a frank and, for the times, scandalous treatment of delicate matters could not be published. The "characters" were all real and well known: Jean le Rond d'Alembert (1717–1783), mathematician and philosopher; Julie de L'Espinasse (1732–1776), hostess of one of the leading *salons* of Paris; and Dr. Théophile de Bordeu (1722–1776), distinguished for his research on the behavior of the pulse. A few copies of the manuscript were made and circulated privately; then, somehow, reports of them reached Mademoiselle de L'Espinasse. Shocked at learning of the opinions attributed to her in the *Dream,* she demanded that all the manuscripts be destroyed. Diderot reluctantly complied. By chance one copy survived and eventually made its way into the archives of Catherine of Russia. It is from this copy that the first printed edition (1830) and all subsequent editions of *D'Alembert's Dream* have been made.

Darwin's Bulldog

The name given to the brilliant biologist Thomas Henry Huxley (1825–1895), for his outspoken championship and defense of Charles Darwin's theory of evolution, after the latter published his *Origin of Species* in 1859.

"Where there was strife there was Huxley," remarked the Irish historian and politician Justin McCarthy (1830–1912), a statement amply borne out by the controversy over Darwin's ideas and Huxley's tireless defense of the man and his thesis. Huxley had received training in both medicine and biological research; but not until he read *Origin of Species* did he find a satisfactory scientific explanation for the transmutation of species. The theory burst upon him like "a flash of light," and he could only exclaim, "How exceedingly stupid not to have thought of that."

Darwin's book had been out scarcely a year when it was assailed by the Bishop of Oxford, the mathematician Samuel Wilberforce (1805–1873) at a meeting of the British Association for the Advancement of Science (affectionately known as the British Ass). Notice of the Bishop's intentions had packed the hall in large part with his sympathizers. Basking in their approval, Wilberforce had spoken glibly and without substance for half an hour, when he made the mistake of inquiring whether Huxley claimed descent from monkeys through his grandfather or his grandmother. Huxley, who was sharing the platform with the Bishop and others, needed no further opening. Speaking with dignity, Huxley quietly and thoroughly dissected his opponent, and concluded, as he later wrote to a friend, "If the question is put whether I would rather have a miserable ape for a grandfather or a man highly endowed by nature and the possessor of great means of influence yet who employs those faculties and that influence for the mere purpose of introducing ridicule into a grave scientific discussion, I unhesitatingly affirm my preference for the apes." At which, Huxley added, the men applauded and the ladies fluttered their handkerchiefs.

Another adversary was Sir Richard Owen, Director of the Hunterian and later of the British Museum, who indignantly disputed the finding of similarities between the brains of gorilla and man. Huxley found the encounters vastly stimulating. Get on with your work, he told Darwin, and leave the wrestling to me; Darwin meekly obeyed.

If the clash with Wilberforce and Fundamentalism was Huxley's sharpest, the one with Prime Minister Gladstone (1809–1898) was the lengthiest, for it began in 1885 and lasted a full six years. With advances in geology bolstering the theory of evolution, Gladstone, a seriously religious man, put forward the claim that these scientific discoveries actually affirmed the story of the Creation as found in Genesis. Huxley had been ill for some time, but the prospect of again doing battle for the Theory was better than medicine. After a series of published exchanges, Huxley attacking with all the resources of scientific experience and Gladstone attempting to reconcile the camps of religion and science, the latter ended up in no-man's-land.

But what Huxley sought to demolish was always the error and not the man who fell into it. When a statue to Gladstone was erected at Liverpool, Huxley willingly accepted an invitation to speak at the unveiling, and to pay tribute to his "favorite enemy."

Darwin's Finches

Birds discovered in great numbers on the Galápagos Islands (in the Pacific Ocean about 650 miles west of Ecuador) by Charles Darwin (1809–1882) while on an exploratory voyage on the *Beagle* (1831–1836). They are of particular interest because of the extraordinary number of species, 14 or more, distinguished especially by the sizes and shapes of their bills and by their variegated markings.

Finches are well known in most parts of the world and under a number of names—bullfinch, chaffinch, canary, grosbeak, and so on. Their plumage ranges from somber grays and browns to flashing yellow. What struck Darwin particularly was that the birds he encountered in the Islands bore characteristics he had never seen elsewhere. While noting these, and tabulating especially the differing beak structures from long and slender to short, thick, and conical, he also recorded the diet of the birds and found that it varied correspondingly. Some species ate insects; others, seeds of diverse size and toughness; some fed on cactus; no two species ate the same food.

He evolved no theory at the time, but in October, 1838, after his return to England, he came upon Thomas Malthus (1766–1834) and his *Principle of Population*. Malthus had written that a people in a given area is bound to outgrow its food supply, whereupon starvation, disease, or war will reduce the population to numbers again supportable by agricultural production. It occurred to Darwin that the finches, multiplying unmolested on their isolated islands, had solved their problem in the only possible way: the seed-producing capacity of the land having been outrun, those birds would survive which could find and make use of other foods. Thus a finch with a heavier beak could crack open a harder seed or even a nut; a slender beak could be used to ream out a wood-burrowing insect until then unreachable. What was at first a random variation would be strengthened in succeeding generations as those who possessed the variation survived and the others died off. The variation in plumage, on the other hand, Darwin attributed simply to changes in diet, a speculation borne out, for example, by the fact that the feathers of the European bullfinch turn black when the bird is fed nothing but hempseed.

It was as a result of the *Beagle* voyage that Darwin's notion of natural selection began slowly to take shape. During the next 20 years Darwin painstakingly added to his evidence, until in 1859 he felt ready to announce his world-shaking theory on the evolution of species. *See also* Darwin's Bulldog.

Dido's Lament

The beautiful soprano aria from the opera *Dido and Aeneas* by Henry Purcell (*c.* 1659–1695), sung by the despairing Dido just before she stabs herself after having been abandoned by Aeneas.

Dido, meaning "fugitive," was the name bestowed on Elissa of Tyre when, after the murder of her husband Sychaeus by her brother Pygmalion, she fled her native city in Asia Minor. The story is told that having found refuge on the North African coast, she bargained with the local chieftain, Iarbas, for land of her own and was offered "as much as could be covered by an oxhide." Dido took a skin and had it cut into a narrow, continuous spiral. The result was a leather strip long enough to circumscribe an entire hill, at the summit of which she built the citadel Byrsa (from the Greek *bursa,* skin or hide). There the city of Carthage later grew and flourished.

Historians place the founding of Carthage by the Phoenicians at about 850 B.C. But Virgil (70–19 B.C.), in his epic poem, *The Aeneid,* set the date at the time of the Trojan War, about 1200 B.C., so as to make Dido contemporaneous with his hero Aeneas. In the poet's version, Aeneas and his followers, after the fall of Troy, wandered the seas for seven years. One day a great storm drove their ship onto the African shore near Carthage where, shortly after, Aeneas met Dido and the two fell in love. But the romance was soon shattered by a message from Jupiter, bidding the warrior end his dalliance and fulfill his destiny by founding an empire in Italy. While the legendary Dido is said to have killed herself to avoid having to marry Iarbas, Virgil attributes her death to her desertion by Aeneas.

Purcell's music, extremely melodious and of moving simplicity, has a libretto by the English poet laureate and playwright, Nahum Tate (1652–1715). The opera was commissioned in 1689 by the dancing master, Josias Priest, who ran a boarding school for young women in Chelsea, West London; and it was performed there the same year.

Diogenes' Lantern

The lighted lamp with which Diogenes, the Cynic
(404–323 B.C.), in broad daylight, prowled the streets of
Athens looking for "an honest man."

The Cynics, or Dog Philosophers (Greek *kuōn*, dog;
adjective form, *kunikós*), seem to have acquired their de-
scriptive title from the nickname given Diogenes, a founder
of the sect. As crusaders against the corrupting influences
of luxurious living, they were noted for their teachings of
asceticism and strict self-discipline. Diogenes had come to
Athens as a young man from his birthplace in Sinope and
soon began to practice the abstinence for which, as well as
for his sharp tongue, he was to become famous.

The story of his search for an honest man may be
apocryphal, but it well expressed his bitter contempt for
convention and for the acquisitiveness and marketplace
mentality of his fellow men. His idea of happiness was to
possess nothing beyond the barest necessities. A tub gave
him shelter enough; he wore his cloak by day and folded it
to sleep on at night; and he often walked barefoot in the
snow. Once, when captured by pirates and put up for sale,
he was queried as to what he could do. "Govern men," he
replied, and asked to be sold to someone who needed a
master.

The 3rd-century (A.D.) writer Diogenes Laertius
gathered together many of the *chreia* or moral epigrams
with which the Cynic pointed up his teachings. Someone
remarked that life is an evil; "Not life itself," replied Diogenes, "but living ill." Seeing a child drinking water from
its hands, the philosopher threw away his own cup, saying
that the child had outdone him in plain living.

Alexander the Conqueror is said once to have visited
Diogenes. Standing beside him Alexander offered Diogenes
whatever he wished. "Just move out of my light," was the

answer. "If I were not Alexander," the ruler commented later, "I should wish to be Diogenes."

For all their bite, many of the sayings show a wry compassion for the human condition. On being asked the proper time for lunch, Diogenes replied: "If a rich man, when you will; if a poor man, when you can." As to the proper time for marriage, he observed: "For a young man not yet; for an old man never at all." And to the question, "What is wretched in life," he answered, "An old man destitute."

But upon being asked what was the most beautiful thing in the world, he declared, "Freedom of speech."

Dorr's Rebellion

An uprising organized in 1842 by the young Rhode Island lawyer Thomas Wilson Dorr (1805–1854) in protest against the refusal of the state supreme court and United States President John Tyler to recognize the validity of a People's Constitution extending manhood suffrage in Rhode Island.

Half of the adult male population of Rhode Island was disfranchised by strict property qualifications for voting. Between 1796 and 1824 some half-dozen calls for a constitutional convention had gone unheeded by the state administrations. Finally, in 1841, Thomas Wilson Dorr, a Harvard graduate and former member of the legislature, sent out his own call for a People's Convention, without, needless to say, the permission of the state body.

His invitation met with a lively response. In October of that year delegates elected on the principle of universal manhood suffrage met in Providence from the 9th to the 14th to write a People's Constitution. They then adjourned for a month, reconvening on November 15. Three days later they emerged with a document that provided for, among other things, extension of the suffrage, readjustment of representation as between rural towns and the rapidly industrializing cities, and an independent judiciary. The constitution was submitted to a popular vote December 27–29 and approved overwhelmingly.

Stung to action by this show of feeling, the General Assembly met in January to work on a rival constitution. They shunted aside the People's Constitution, and on February 18 read and adopted a so-called Freeman's Constitution. Put to a "popular" vote in March, it lost by a margin of 676.

Following this defeat, on April 1, the Assembly passed an act that made illegal any election taking place without state authority and held anyone assuming office by virtue of such an election guilty of high treason and subject to life imprisonment. This was the Algerine Act, so labeled (by the Providence *Express*) because it resembled the arbitrary decrees of the ancient Deys of Algiers. Undaunted, Dorr went ahead, and at an election later in April was named governor. In reprisal, the regular administration began picking up Dorr adherents under the Algerine Act.

An appeal to the state supreme court brought a ruling that the People's Constitution was invalid. In Washington, D.C., President Tyler refused to intervene. There seemed only one recourse—armed open rebellion. Dorr gathered several hundred Rhode Island stalwarts, and on the night of May 17 launched an attack on the Providence Arsenal. The foray was brief, bloodless, and unsuccessful. By dawn most of the men had dispersed and the Dorr government had resigned. Dorr himself, on the advice of friends, sought temporary refuge outside of the state.

A month later a second attempt to rally his followers having failed, Dorr formally dissolved the movement. Ignoring his dissolution order, the state government declared Dorr a traitor and put a price on his head. The next year a somewhat improved constitution was voted, and Dorr ventured back into Rhode Island. He was promptly arrested and charged with high treason; in 1844 he was tried and sentenced to life at hard labor.

While the citizens might have criticized Dorr's methods, they could only admire his motives. Popular clamor brought him a pardon in 1845. Six years later Dorr's full citizenship rights were restored, and in 1854, shortly before he died, an annulment of the court judgment erased the last vestige of indictment.

Among Dorr's champions was an unknown 23-year-old newspaperman who later became one of America's leading poets. On August 14, 1842, the front page of the New York *Sunday Times* (no relation to today's *Times*) printed a poem in glowing defense of Dorr; entitled "No Turning Back," it was signed W. Whitman. In a nearby column, unsigned but presumed to be by the same W. Whitman, was an "Original Sketch," which outlined and justified in prose what had been sung in verse: "Glorious was the ground on which he stood . . . His motives . . . have been as pure and high as his cause has been just and righteous."

Down's Syndrome
The evidences of mongolism: low, sloping forehead; short, flat-bridged nose; splayed hands and feet with shortened digital bones; moderate to severe mental retardation; physical abnormalities detectable in the embryo. These were identified by the English physician John L. L. Down (1826–1896).

Dr. Eliot's Five-Foot Shelf
The *Harvard Classics,* 50 volumes of the world's outstanding literature, philosophy, poetry, science, and drama, compiled by the noted educator and reformer of higher education, Charles William Eliot (1834–1926), who be-

came president of Harvard in 1869 and served in that office for 40 years.

The proposal that Eliot edit a library of classics was brought to him—by Norman Hapgood and William Patten of Collier's—soon after he had announced his resignation from the presidency of Harvard. Just fifteen minutes of reading each day from the "shelf," he declared, would in time amount to a liberal education.

The idea aroused enormous interest. Even before there was any mention of the contents of the volumes, "editorial writers and people who write letters to the press," observed Henry James in his biography of Eliot, set themselves to commenting on both the impressiveness of the undertaking and the difficulty in carrying it out; "no Sunday supplement or book section was complete without some one's discussion of Dr. Eliot's books."

To assist him in compiling the library, Eliot called on William Allan Neilson, then at Harvard, later president of Smith College. Working on huge sheets of paper, Professor Neilson first laid out the centuries in the left-hand column, then filled in successive columns with pertinent events, discoveries, topics, and so on. With an age or period sketched in, appropriate literature to explain and interpret it was selected.

Once published, the Five-Foot Shelf achieved a popularity that surprised even its creators, although jokes were made about the prescriptive fifteen minutes a day. It was hard to dismiss a Shelf that included Franklin's and Cellini's autobiographies, Plutarch's *Lives*, Dante's *Divine Comedy*, Darwin's *Origin of Species*, Mill and Carlyle, Faraday and Helmholtz, Descartes and Hobbes, Luther, Locke, Berkeley, Hume, Harvey, Pasteur and dozens more.

"The best acquisition of a cultivated man," Eliot had written, "is a liberal frame of mind"; with the *Harvard Clas-*

sics he sought to make that acquisition possible for the greatest number.

Eratosthenes' Sieve

(Eratosthenes' net). A method devised by Eratosthenes of Alexandria (*c.* 276–*c.* 192 B.C.) for screening out the prime numbers from the series of whole numbers.

Prime numbers are those integers, greater than 1, which have the special property of being evenly divisible only by themselves and 1. From the time they were first noticed by Pythagoras in the 6th century B.C. to the present, prime numbers have given rise to a considerable body of theorems describing their peculiar attributes and their behavior within the number system.

One question in particular has always challenged the number enthusiasts: Is there some formula or algorithm by which we can determine whether any given number is a prime or which will generate an indefinite series of primes?

Eratosthenes was the first to devise a method for sifting out primes. He began by writing down the integers, starting with 1. Then he crossed out all even numbers except 2 (itself a prime by definition) and all multiples of 3 except 3 (for the same reason). The next number after 3, both odd and prime, is 5; and the one after that is 7. By canceling all multiples first of 5 and then of 7, all non-primes up through 120 are screened out. Thus each prime takes its turn as a "sifter." The next sifter is 11; notice that the number on which it begins its operation is 121 or 11^2. When 13 is reached, all non-primes will have been taken out up to its own square of 169. The next prime, 17, comes into use at 289, or 17^2, and so on.

Eratosthenes left no writings that specifically mention his sieve; the first account of it comes from Nichomachus of Greece, about 100 A.D. After that a succession of scholars tackled the problem of enlarging the number of known primes.

As of 1963, the largest known prime was $2^{11213}-1$. Multiplied out, it has 3,376 digits (the equivalent of about 400 lines of type on an average page). Yet the computer which "found" the prime was programmed to nothing more sophisticated than the cancellation method of Eratosthenes.

Fermat's Last Theorem

(Fermat's lost theorem). That there is no non-zero solution in integers for the equation $a^n+b^n=c^n$, where n is greater than 2.

Mathematics was only the avocation of Pierre de Fermat (1601–1665). Educated for the law, he spent many years as a counselor of parliament at Toulouse, but used his spare time brilliantly in the field of pure mathematics.

Fermat was in the habit of making notes on the margins of the treatises he happened to be reading. When marginal space was limited, he would simply set down his own results on a problem without including the steps of the proof. It happened that one day, probably in 1637, he was studying the *Arithmetica* of Diophantus of Alexandria (fl. 250 A.D.), a work that dealt largely with the behavior of numbers squared, cubed, or raised to higher powers. While mulling over the fact, discussed in Book II, that certain squares are the sum of two other squares, for example, $5^2(25) = 3^2(9) + 4^2(16)$, Fermat noted in the margin: "On the contrary, it is impossible to separate a cube into two cubes, a fourth power into two fourth powers, or, generally, any power above the second into two powers of the same degree: I have discovered a truly marvelous demonstration which this margin is too narrow to contain."

That was all. M. Fermat never published his "marvelous demonstration," nor has any trace of a general proof, for all integer values of n greater than 2, been found among his papers. He did prove his theorem for $n = 4$, i.e., that there is no solution for the equation $a^4 + b^4 = c^4$, and a century later Leonhard Euler proved that there is none for $n = 3$. By the middle of the 19th century the same had been done for $n = 5$, and $n = 7$. Finally, during the 1950s, computers were put to work on the problem. Through calculations made on SWAC (Standards Western Automatic Computer, located at the University of California, Los Angeles), the theorem has been verified for all exponents up to $n = 4,000$. But a general proof, which Fermat might have recorded had the margin been a bit wider, still eludes even the most sophisticated mathematical methods.

Fingal's Cave

A huge cavern on the northern coast of Staffa (a small island of the Inner Hebrides), discovered and described in 1772 by Sir Joseph Banks (1743–1820). It is said to have been a refuge for the semimythological figure of Gaelic folklore, Finn MacCumhaill (Finn MacCool).

"Suppose the Giants who rebelled against Jove," wrote John Keats to his brother Tom in July, 1818, "had taken a whole Mass of Black Columns and bound them together like bunches of matches—and then with immense axes had made a cavern in the body of these columns . . . such is Fingal's cave."

A decade or so later Felix Mendelssohn was equally moved by the sight. "In order to make you understand how extraordinarily the Hebrides affected me," he wrote in a letter home (August 7, 1829), "the following came into my mind . . . ," and then he had set down on hand-drawn staves some twenty bars of the rippling introduction to his *Hebrides Overture*.

Like the Blue Grotto at Capri, Fingal's Cave can be

entered only by boat; but once within it is possible to walk along the sides of the cave on broken rock slabs. The lofty, six-sided pillars are of volcanic origin, part of an early flow that moved from Iceland through the Hebrides to the northern coast of Ireland, where the same pillar formation seems to march out of the sea and come to a halt in County Antrim. At this southern end the columns are known as the Giant's Causeway; and legend has it that at one time they supported one end of a roadway running from the north Irish coast to the island of Staffa and built by a race of giants.

The cave itself was discovered by Sir Joseph Banks in August, 1772, while sailing along the mythical route of the Causeway on a voyage to Iceland. The sight of it threw him into raptures, not only for the beauty of the place but for the host of heroic associations it called up. "How fortunate," he wrote later, "that in this cave we should meet with the remembrance of that chief whose existence as well as that of the whole epick poem is almost doubted in England."

That "chief," in Sir Joseph's spelling, was "Fiuhn Mac Coul, whoom the translator of Ossian's works has called Fingal." Finn was probably a general under King Cormac mac Airt of Tara, responsible for organizing the army of the third century Irish ruler. As time went on, fancy embroidered fact, and in both Ireland and Scotland a body of folklore grew up around the brawny leader and his merry band of warriors, who roamed about defending Ireland from hostile invaders. Their exploits were said to have been put into bardic verse by Ossian or Oisin (pronounced Usheen), a son of Finn.

Ford's Peace Ship

The *Oscar II,* chartered during World War I by the
automobile manufacturer, Henry Ford (1863–1947), to
take a group of liberals and pacifists on a peace crusade to
Europe in December of 1915, under the slogan, "Get the
boys out of the trenches by Christmas."

Ford's involvement in opposition to the war seems to
have begun in the spring of 1915. At first he made state-
ments to the press denouncing the conflict in bitterest terms.
This was a capitalists' war, he said, brought on by the
money lenders and Wall Street parasites; later, naming
names, he castigated Morgan and Company for its half-
billion dollar loan to the Allies. As for himself, if the war
spread to the United States, he would burn his factory to
the ground rather than fill an order for cars that might be
put to military use.

The idea for translating his sentiments into action was
the outcome of a long interview that fall with the Hun-
garian journalist and suffrage organizer, Rosika Schwimmer. Madame Schwimmer, together with Mrs. Pethick Lawrence, a British pacifist, was touring this country in behalf
of an international peace movement whose aims were twofold: to discuss reasonable terms of peace, and to protest
against war as a means of settling international difficulties.
When the subject of a Conference of Neutrals to be held in
some nonbelligerent country was broached to him, Ford
declared his willingness to finance such a plan. In a conference with President Wilson shortly thereafter, Ford was
assured that the private financing of such an undertaking
would not embarrass the government, although Wilson himself, to Ford's chagrin, gave no personal endorsement.

Back in New York, Ford went ahead with his plans for
the expedition, apparently without any appreciable consultation with the committee of the Women's Peace Party
which was organizing the American delegation. Jane Ad-

dams (1860–1935), chairman of the newly formed party, was particularly disturbed at the announcement of the chartered vessel, feeling that the delegates would have been quite satisfied to make their own arrangements and pay their own way. "We needed Mr. Ford's help primarily in organizing a conference," she wrote later (*Peace and Bread in Time of War*), "but not in transporting the people." Disputes also arose over the invitation list. Ford wanted to do the inviting himself, and a flood of invitations went out. Many of them were to "honest, devoted and also distinguished people," Miss Addams commented; but such an expenses-paid journey was bound to attract, as it did, "many fanatic and impecunious reformers" as well.

The newspapers missed no opportunity to play up whatever was bizarre or could be made to look so, and the chorus of ridicule grew. Serious delegates were becoming increasingly uncomfortable. It seemed as if Ford's facile "Out of the trenches by Christmas" was pushing the Conference of Neutrals and its purpose into the background. Then a number of the more distinguished invitees began wiring regrets. Jane Addams was genuinely ill in Chicago, but many others, including Thomas Edison and the naturalist John Burroughs, whom Ford considered among his closest friends, politely declined.

Despite all adversities, the *Oscar II* finally left New York for Christiania, Norway. From there the delegates went to Stockholm, where the Conference was formally set up on January 26, 1916, with five representatives each from Sweden, Norway, Denmark, Holland, and Switzerland, and three from the United States. By Easter their deliberations had produced a powerful appeal directed to "the Governments, Parliaments and People of Belligerent Nations," which embodied a wide spectrum of national viewpoints garnered both by letter and by personal testimony. In spirit and in much of its substance the document foreshadowed what would appear some three years later as the Fourteen Points (*see* Wilson's Fourteen Points).

Ford did not stay for the parley. Confined to his stateroom with a heavy cold for much of the trip, he went to bed on arrival, and a few days later, under the pressure of several friends who had opposed the entire venture, sailed for home. He maintained an interest in the Conference, however, contributing a subsidy of 10,000 dollars a month for about a year. In January, 1917, reflecting a change in public opinion, his enthusiasm began to wane. A month later he announced that his support for the conference would end March 1. When war was declared on April 6 his pacifism dissolved. By October he was urging everyone to "back our Uncle Samuel with a shotgun loaded to the muzzle with buckshot."

Ford's Theatre

The playhouse on 10th Street, N.W., Washington, D.C., owned by John T. Ford, where President Abraham Lincoln (1809–1865) was assassinated on Friday night, April 14, 1865, by the actor and Confederate sympathizer John Wilkes Booth (1838–1865).

The play that night was the comedy *Our American Cousin*. The star was the English-born actress Laura Keene. In flag-draped Box 7 were the President and Mrs. Lincoln, their son Tad, Major Henry R. Rathbone, and the latter's fiancée, Clara Harris, daughter of Senator Ira Harris of New York. With the Civil War formally ended the week before (April 9), Lincoln and his family were spending the first relatively carefree evening in four long years.

Entrance for Booth, a younger brother of the more celebrated actor Edwin Booth (1833–1893), was ridiculously easy. The President's bodyguard, John J. Parker, after inspecting the box and settling the party, went next door to

Taltavul's Tavern for a drink. Booth saw him come in and moved quickly. The events that followed—the single pistol-shot, the 14-foot leap to the stage, the shout "Sic semper tyrannis," and the assassin's ignominious death two weeks later in a country barn—are well known.

The national tragedy put an end to the playhouse. The government immediately confiscated it: and, although Ford moved to reclaim it in July of that summer and had actually scheduled a play, *The Octoroon,* public indignation demanded and got enforcement of the original ban. Eventually the whole interior, balconies, boxes, and all, was torn out and the theater refurbished as an office building. Subsequently it served as an Army medical museum, an office, a storage place. In 1893 the third floor collapsed, killing 22 workers. Taken over by the Park Service in 1932, the building became a Lincoln Museum.

In the fall of 1967 a plan was announced to restore the theater. Fortunately, photographs of the old interior were available; they had been taken shortly after the assassination night by Matthew Brady and Alexander Gardner for possible use in investigating the crime. Working from these, architects and decorators recreated the 42-foot stage, the graceful high proscenium arch, and the white-plaster balconies. There has been a change in the seating arrangements —the old house had a capacity of 1,700, which modern fire regulations have reduced to 600—and the gas lights have been replaced with electric bulbs and reflectors. Only the first floor is now being used as a playhouse. The second floor has been set aside for special programs, while the third houses a 2,500-volume Lincoln library, including some books that had belonged to the President.

On January 21, 1968, the restored theater was dedicated "to the arts . . . and to the American people." On February 12, a new resident National Repertory Company gave its opening performance of Stephen Vincent Benét's *John Brown's Body*.

Foucault's Pendulum

A pendulum consisting of a heavy weight on a long wire which, when set swinging to and fro, gradually appears to change the direction of its swing. It was used in 1851 by the French physicist Léon Foucault (1819–1868) to demonstrate the rotation of the earth.

Foucault's first experiment, described in a paper presented to the French Academy of Sciences in February, 1851, took place in a vaulted cellar "whose arch offered an especially rigid support." The pendulum, a brass sphere weighing about 11 pounds hung on a thin steel wire some 6½ feet long, was attached to a steel plate in the ceiling. After the device had been swinging for a period of time, the deviation of its apparent line of swing from the initial line was clearly evident.

A reproduction of Foucault's pendulum may be seen today in the National Academy of Sciences in Washington, D.C. A hollow, gold-plated ball, 15 inches in diameter and weighing about 240 pounds, is suspended from a 73-foot flexible steel cable clamped in a circular vise at the top of the building. Every morning at 9 A.M. a golden pointer set into the floor below the pendulum is lined up with the pendulum swing. As the day goes on, the rotation of the earth carries the floor with its pointer away from the line of swing in a clockwise motion.

Fox's "Martyrs"

The 160 followers of Charles James Fox (1749–1806), a former secretary of state under George III of England, who lost their Parliamentary seats in the general elections of 1784 as a result of the political struggle between

Fox and William Pitt, the Younger, newly appointed Prime Minister. The expression Fox's "martyrs" involves a play on words, the reference being to John Foxe's *Book of Martyrs* (published in four editions from 1554 to 1583), an exhaustive history covering two centuries of English men and women who had suffered persecution and death, often by burning at the stake, for their religious faith.

Fulton's Folly

The *Clermont,* one of the earliest steam-driven vessels, built by the Pennsylvania-born Robert Fulton (1765–1815), which on a three-day trial run on the Hudson River, from New York to Albany and back, provided the first successful demonstration of the steamboat.

When Robert Fulton, as a little boy, was scolded for not attending to his schoolbooks, he is said to have answered gravely that his head was too full of his own ideas to have room for what was between dusty covers. Unusually talented, he could paint a portrait, draw plans for machinery, and design a building with equal skill; and he had done all three with some success before he was twenty.

In 1786 he went to London, where he renewed acquaintance with, and for a while studied under, a friend of his childhood, the American painter Benjamin West (1738–1820). For the next several years Fulton painted and exhibited; he met the Duke of Bridgewater and the Earl of Stanhope, and as a result became interested in canal transport and navigation by steam. In 1794 Fulton took out British patents on a device for raising and lowering canal boats, on a flax spinning machine, and on a new way of twisting hemp rope.

At the same time plans were taking shape for the practical use of steam to propel water vessels. The ideals of the French Revolution had stirred Fulton deeply, and his own thoughts, directed toward the "Universal betterment of Humanity," led him to sketch out a constructive system of canals and a destructive system of torpedoes to insure freedom of the waterways, by force if necessary. Invited to France in 1801 by the American Minister Robert R. Livingston, Fulton began experiments there on a "plunging boat"; he descended to a depth of 25 feet in Brest harbor and stayed under for an hour. The following year, on the Seine, he launched a boat that moved by steam-driven paddle wheels and drew two other boats behind it.

Satisfied that he had produced a workable craft, Fulton in 1806 left Paris for New York. Here he set to work on a vessel that could be put to practical use. The shipbuilder Charles Brown was entrusted with construction of the hull. A steam engine was ordered from the English firm of Boulton and Watt, but delivery was maddeningly delayed until the British government decided to let it out of the country. In the meantime the mysterious goings-on behind closed doors in the shed near the river were jeered at as Fulton's folly; Fulton himself was running out of cash. The last 1,000 dollars was borrowed from friends who made him promise not to reveal their names.

On August 7, 1807, with flags flying, the *Clermont,* named in honor of Minister Livingston's estate, left its dock at 10th Street in New York City and steamed up the Hudson, bound for Albany 150 miles away. The run was made in 32 hours, the return trip in 30, with not a single incident to mar the record. "The power of propelling boats by steam," stated Fulton jubilantly, "is now fully proved."

Godey's Lady's Book

An American magazine for women founded in 1830 by Louis Antoine Godey (1804–1878), containing stories, fashions, recipes, household hints, and the like. It merged in 1837 with Sarah Josepha Hale's *Ladies' Magazine* (founded in 1828) and continued publication until 1898 after the death of both founders in the late 1870s.

The first two successful magazines devoted solely to women and women's interests appeared almost simultaneously. The earlier one was founded and edited by a woman, the first of her sex to do so. Widowed after nine years of marriage and with five children to support, Sarah Josepha Hale (1788–1879), then living in Boston, determined upon a publication that would educate as well as entertain. To this end she sought for her *Ladies' Magazine,* in addition to stories and book reviews, a variety of original contributions on such thought-provoking topics as social reform, health, and morals. When contributors were in short supply she wrote many of the articles herself.

Godey's magazine, on the other hand, was cast in a lighter vein; stories, poems, and songs were interspersed with dress and embroidery patterns, and colored plates of the latest fashions in dresses and bonnets. A self-educated man, Godey had worked for a time in a New York broker's office, then opened a book store and circulating library. In 1828 he moved to Philadelphia; two years later he began to publish *Godey's Lady's Book.*

The merger of the two magazines in 1837 brought together the best features of each. At first called *Lady's Book and American Ladies' Magazine,* the publication later assumed Godey's original title, although the force of the co-editor's personality caused it often to be referred to as "Mrs. Hale's magazine." Lively and scrupulously up-to-date on many issues, the monthly attracted articles by such figures as Horace Greeley, Charles Beecher, and Harriet Beecher Stowe; printed a series of six essays by Edgar Allen Poe on "Literary Criticism" in 1846; and carried reviews of works by Poe, Melville, and Prescott.

Mrs. Hale's interests were widespread and her opinions

definite. She recorded her approval of intelligent philan-
thropy and her opposition to dueling; founded, through
her magazine, the first Seamen's Aid Society; supported a
movement to assist a female seminary in Liberia; agitated
for supplanting men teachers by women in all but the highest schools, and supported training for women doctors. Mrs.
Hale was concerned with economic opportunities for
women, and she made a proud point of the fact that in the
early 1850s the magazine employed between 90 and 100
women in coloring, binding, and other departments.

She was not a feminist in the full sense of the word.
The women's rights movement as such was never cham-
pioned by *Godey's*. The magazine was content to follow
faithfully the line laid down in Mrs. Hale's first editorial
after the merger—that woman's sphere of power lies in the
domain of moral sentiment!

Goldbach's Conjecture(s)

The hypotheses that every even number from 6 on
could be represented as the sum of two odd primes, and
following from this, that every odd number from 9 on could
be represented as the sum of three odd primes were advanced in 1742 by the German mathematician Christian
Goldbach (1690–1764) in a series of letters to the celebrated Swiss mathematician Leonhard Euler (1707–1783).
(For more on primes, *see* Eratosthenes' sieve).

Goldbach was in Russia as Secretary of the Academy of
Sciences at St. Petersburg and Euler in Berlin as a member
of the Academy of Sciences there, when the correspondence on the conjectures was initiated. Every case he had
tried so far, Goldbach wrote, seemed to prove that his conjectures were correct. Could Euler furnish him with the
certainty either that they were true, or were not true, for all
the natural numbers? Euler replied that while he thought

they were true, he was unable to find any proof. Nor did he ever.

If we begin as Goldbach did, we will find it easy enough to verify the conjectures for individual numbers. For example: $6 = 3 + 3, 8 = 3 + 5, 10 = 3 + 7, \ldots; 9 = 3 + 3 + 3, 11 = 3 + 3 + 5, 13 = 3 + 5 + 5$, and so on. Or there may be more than one combination that satisfies the requirement of only two primes for the even numbers, three for the odd: $28 = 17 + 11$ and also $23 + 5; 39 = 5 + 11 + 23$ and also $7 + 13 + 19$. Of course when we get to the larger numbers, the thousands, ten thousands, and up, the work of verification becomes quite tedious. But, mathematically speaking, *verification* of specific instances, no matter how many, is not *proof* of generalizations such as the conjectures. Here, proof must take the form of a procedure or formula applicable to all instances, in this case all the natural numbers.

Goldbach's first conjecture has been verified numerically up to 100,000. As for proof, the first important advance came in 1931, when a young Russian mathematician proved that "every positive integer can be represented as the sum of not more than 300,000 primes," rather a farout figure compared with the original conjecture but headed in the right direction. Six years later another Russian, I. M. Vinogradov, produced an indirect proof which, for "sufficiently large" numbers, brought that total down to at most four primes for the first conjecture and to three for the second, thus "solving" the latter. But his result does not allow us to pinpoint "sufficiently large."

The first conjecture, however, (any even number as the sum of two primes) still remains impregnable.

Graves's Disease

Characterized by goiter, or enlargement of the thyroid gland (hyperthyroidism), leading to an increase in basal metabolism (burning up of body carbons, proteins, and fats), loss of weight, and extreme nervousness. Another symptom is exophthalmos ("pop-eyes") due to pressure from the enlarged thyroid. The disease is curable by the use of radioactive iodine or by surgery and was first described by the Irish physician Robert Graves (1796–1853).

Gresham's Law

The name suggested in 1858 by the Scottish economist, Henry Dunning Macleod (1821–1902), for the economic principle that when a debased coinage is introduced into circulation alongside a true coinage, the latter will disappear from the market place; that is, "bad money drives out good."

The suggestion that Sir Thomas Gresham (1519–1579), a London merchant and founder of the Royal Exchange, be given credit for this "law" is found near the end of Macleod's *Elements of Political Economy* (London, 1858). In Chapter VI, "Sketch of the History of the Currency of England," he cites a letter from Gresham to Queen Elizabeth shortly after her accession in 1558, pointing out that debasement of coinage by Henry VIII was the cause for the disappearance of the good coin of the realm. The *fact* that good money disappears in the presence of bad money, said Macleod, had been noted many times before, as early as Aristophanes and as late as contemporary English writers; but "Sir Thomas Gresham, we believe, was the first . . . to perceive that a bad and debased currency is the *cause* of the disappearance of good money," and for this reason "we are only doing what is just in calling this great fundamental law of currency by his name. We may call it Gresham's law of the currency."

Gresham was not the first to discover this relationship, and Macleod later corrected himself. In a pamphlet written in 1895 for the Gold Standard Defense Association, a British organization to combat bimetallism, Macleod included a summary of that part of Chapter VI dealing with debasement. Noting that his 1858 suggestion of Gresham's name for the law "has now been universally accepted," Macleod added that he had not been aware until 1864 of two earlier formulations identical in thought to Gresham's. One was by the French scientist and churchman Nicole Oresme (c. 1325–1382) in a report to Charles V of France (1366), in which he said that when coin is debased, gold and silver "are carried out to places where they are rated higher"; the other by the Polish astronomer Nicolaus Copernicus (1473–1543), who, in addition to disproving the Ptolemaic theory of the solar system, expressed substantially the same idea as Oresme in an exposition of the principles of currency reform written in 1525 and first published in Warsaw in 1816.

Since there is no reason to suppose that Sir Thomas knew of these two previous works, Macleod continues, it would seem that all three arrived independently at the same conclusion and that the principle should really be renamed the Law of Oresme, Copernicus, and Gresham.

Grimm's Law

A pattern of phonological or sound changes that took place in the Germanic languages as they became separated from their Indo-European ancestors; named for the "father of modern philology," the German scholar Jacob Grimm (1785–1863) of fairytale fame.

Grimm's law is actually not a law, and the first investiga-

tions into sound changes were made not by Jacob Grimm
but by the Danish philologist Rasmus Kristian Rask (1787–
1832). Rask had been at work tracing the affinity of Ice-
landic to other Indo-European languages, and in 1818
published an essay on the origin of the Scandinavian
tongue.

Perhaps inspired by Rask's essay, which is especially
referred to in the preface, Grimm a year later brought out
his *Deutsche Grammatik,* a comparative grammar of all
the Germanic languages—Gothic, Scandinavian, English,
Frisian, Dutch, and German. A second edition in 1822
set forth in systematic detail the correspondence of consonants between the Germanic and other Indo-European
languages that has come to be known as Grimm's law.

A few examples of the shift between Latin and English
illustrate the pattern of changes discovered by Rask and
Grimm: p becomes f (Latin *pes,* English *foot*), t becomes
th (*trēs, three*), d becomes t (*duo, two*), g becomes k,
or hard c (*granum, corn*), k becomes h (*cornu, horn*).

Gull's Disease

Myxedema or atrophy of the thyroid gland (hypothy-
roidism), marked by puffy skin of the face and body, increase in weight, very low basal metabolism, irritability,
and a slowing down of mental activity. It often affects
members of the same family, transmitted by the mother,
women being six times as susceptible as men. The disease,
relieved by doses of thyroid extract, was first observed in
1873 by the English physician Sir William Gull (1816–
1890).

Halley's Comet

First observed in 1682 by the London-born astronomer Edmund Halley (1656–1742) and made the subject of

calculations, later confirmed, by which he proved its perio-
dicity and thus established for the first time that comets do
return to the solar system.

> ". . . Now we know
> The sharply veering ways of comets, once
> A source of dread, nor longer do we quail
> Beneath appearances of bearded stars."
> —EDMUND HALLEY, PREFACE TO VOL. I, *Principia*
> by Isaac Newton

Halley's observations of the "bearded stars"—the word,
comet, is from the Greek *kometes* meaning "long-haired"—
had begun in 1680. Something of a mathematical prodigy,
he was already known for his astronomical studies and was
barely twenty when his first paper on the orbits of planets
was published by the Royal Society in 1676. Having noted
certain discrepancies between the theoretically plotted orbits
of Jupiter and Saturn and the ones they were observed to
travel, he spent the next 18 months below the equator on
the little British island of St. Helena, in order to verify his
data from another latitude. On his return to England, he
was awarded a master's degree at Oxford and in that
same year (1678) first made Newton's acquaintance.

Newton in earlier calculations of planetary orbits had
confirmed the elliptical paths of planets. Now he suggested
that comets too might move in ellipses (so enormously
elongated that a complete circuit would take more than a
man's lifetime). Making use of this hypothesis, Halley set
about computing the orbit of a comet that had appeared in
1682 and went on to a detailed study of all the known data
on cometary phenomena. During the next two decades he
collected enough material to work out the orbits of 24
comets back to 1337. Analysis of his figures showed that
the comets of 1531, 1607, and the one of 1682 seemed to
be traveling in almost identical paths, and he surmised that
the three were really one. Further examination revealed

similar behavior by the comet of 1456. With this additional evidence, Halley concluded that this comet had an orbital period of approximately 75½ years and predicted another appearance sometime in 1758 or 1759. His prediction was fulfilled. Halley's comet reached its next perihelion (closest approach to the sun and therefore to the earth) on March 13, 1759, and the periodic return of comets was established beyond the shadow of a doubt.

Since Halley's time, and on the basis of his figures, more than thirty appearances of his comet have been identified, ranging from the first in 467 B.C. to the latest in 1910. The ancients dreaded these fiery apparitions as messengers of catastrophe, and the superstition persists. Curiously enough, the advent of Halley's comet often seemed to coincide with disaster: the war in 66 A.D. that brought about the fall of Jerusalem; the devastation of Italy by the Huns in 373 A.D.; the Battle of Hastings in 1066—it is Halley's comet that is woven into the panel of the Bayeux tapestry depicting the death of Harold at the hands of William the Conqueror.

Our own century has not been immune to the old apprehensions. For days in advance, the anticipated visit of the comet in 1910 was front-page news, and excitement mounted with the approach of May 18, the date when the earth was to pass through the comet's tail. People expected the seas to boil and the land to be scorched and blistered. A group of French astronomers published their fears that the gases in the tail would poison the earth's atmosphere. As the dreaded day drew nearer there were reports of temporary insanity and attempted suicides; anticomet pills, guaranteeing protection, were sold at a dollar a box.

Overflow crowds attended lectures at Columbia University, where they were told that at its closest the comet would be 14 million miles from the earth; that its head was not solid but formed of glowing gases and minute bits of meteoric matter; and that the 24 million-mile tail was so delicate and unsubstantial that its only effect on earth might be some minor electrical disturbances.

Halley's "bearded star" is due again in 1986.

Hansen's Disease

The dreaded leprosy referred to in the bible, widespread in medieval times, and first described clinically in 1874 by the Norwegian physician Gerhard Armauer Hansen. It is caused by the microorganism *Mycobacterium leprae,* sometimes called Hansen's bacillus.

Leprosy is a chronic disease found under conditions of filth and poor diet. It may be communicated by prolonged direct contact, children being especially susceptible. There are two types of the disease: neural (or maculo-anesthetic), where the skin changes color, loses feeling, and ulcerates, and the hands often are deformed into claws; and cutaneous (or lepromatous), in which the skin thickens and develops nodules, and, where the face is affected, the features are altered to a lionlike appearance. The two types may also be present in the same individual.

While declining everywhere, leprosy is still found in such areas as Latin America, some Pacific islands, and in the Gulf States of the United States.

Harper's Ferry

A town in Jefferson County, West Virginia, at the juncture of the Potomac and Shenandoah rivers, about 55 miles northwest of Washington, D.C.; also a ferry at that point (from which the town drew its name), opened in 1747 by the English-born architect and millwright Robert Harper (1703–1782). The town was the scene of the raid on the government arsenal by the abolitionist John Brown and his followers on October 16, 1859.

Not too much is known of the man whose name is linked with one of the most memorable events in American history. Robert Harper was born in Oxford, England, and emigrated to Philadelphia when he was 20. For a number of years he seems to have plied his trade as architect and builder in various places; a Protestant Episcopal church in Frankfort has been credited to him.

In 1747 he was commissioned by some members of the Society of Friends to build a church on the Opequon river, near where Winchester, Virginia, is now located. On his way there he stopped overnight at a tavern near the present site of Frederick, Maryland, and struck up an acquaintance with a German named Hoffman, who told him about a short cut by way of a place called "The Hole."

"The Hole" turned out to be a magnificent spit of land where the Shenandoah flows into the Potomac, part of a huge estate belonging to Lord Thomas Fairfax (who gave George Washington his first big surveying job). Harper fell in love with the place, and, after some negotiations involving first a squatter named Peter Stevens and later Lord Fairfax himself, bought the Stevens "holding" for 50 guineas. There he settled, built the ferry, and later married.

Near the end of Washington's second administration, in 1796, Harper's Ferry was chosen to be the site of the National Armory, supposedly after a personal visit by the President. This was the arsenal captured on the night of October 16, 1859, by John Brown and about a score of men, five of them Negroes. Brown had planned to set up a refuge in the Virginia mountains for fugitive slaves and stock it with weapons and ammunition for their defense.

His raid was a complete surprise. The arsenal was easily occupied and 60 of the town's citizens were taken as hostages, but the following day the building was surrounded by the local militia, soon joined by a marine force under

Colonel Robert E. Lee. A fierce battle on October 18 left ten of the little band dead, including two of Brown's sons (seven other men were captured; five escaped), and Brown himself was badly wounded. A trial at the end of the month resulted in conviction of the survivors for "treason . . . conspiring . . . advising with slaves and rebels, and murder in the first degree." Early in December all were hanged.

Considered a strategic area, Harper's Ferry changed hands several times during the Civil War. It finally ended up in Northern hands after the Battle of Gettysburg.

Hercules' Club

A spiny-leaved shrub or smallish ornamental tree of the ginseng family, from 10 to 40 feet high, common to the central Eastern seaboard, South, and Southwestern United States. It is also known as prickly ash, angelica tree, or devil's walking stick. The club carried by the mythological Hercules (Heracles) was made of none of these, it seems, but was hewn from a stout branch of wild olive.

Hercules' Labors (Greek Heracles)

Twelve seemingly impossible tasks (originally ten), which the Greek hero Heracles was ordered to perform for Eurystheus, King of Mycenae.

Son of the god Zeus and the mortal Alcmene, Heracles had been foreordained by his divine father to become the greatest of heroes and ruler "of all the sons of Peleus" (the Myceneans). On the day Alcmene was to give birth, Zeus vowed that the first male child born on that day would grow up to be a hero and a ruler. Hera, angered at this latest of her husband's infidelities, used her magic powers to delay Heracles' birth and at the same time hasten that of the child expected by the wife of King Sthenelus of Mycenae. Trapped by his vow as to the kingship, Zeus won a compromise when Hera agreed that Heracles might be admitted to immortality if, when grown to manhood, he performed ten labors to be set by Eurystheus.

These labors were:

1. To slay the Nemean lion, a beast which could not be harmed by iron, bronze, or stone. Heracles strangled the animal, skinned and tanned the pelt, and thereafter wore it as a cloak, using the head as a helmet.

2. To kill the hundred-headed Hydra, which lived in the Lernean swamp and devastated the countryside with its fiery breath. As fast as Heracles severed one head, two grew in its place. Seeing no progress at this rate, Heracles called upon his nephew Iolaus to apply a torch of burning pitch to each stump as a head was struck off, and so destroyed the monster.

3. To capture a wild boar that lived on Mount Erymanthus and ravaged the countryside. Heracles chased the boar northward until it became bogged down in a snowdrift, then threw a net around it, hoisted it on his shoulders, and carried it back to Eurystheus. On learning of Heracles' success Eurystheus was so frightened that he took refuge in a large bronze vessel buried in the courtyard, cautiously raising the lid to peep out at the approaching hero, a scene later reproduced many times in caricature by Greek vase makers.

4. To capture the golden-horned hind which, being sacred to Artemis, had to be taken alive. After a year of pursuit, as the hind paused to drink from a stream, Heracles pierced its forefeet with a single arrow. Artemis rebuked him for doing hurt to the beautiful animal but relented when she learned that this was a labor commanded by Zeus.

5. To drive away the iron-feathered, man-eating birds, sacred to Ares, that lived in the Stymphalian marsh. With a bronze rattle given him by Athena, Heracles roused the

birds to flight and then shot many of them down with his arrows. The rest fled.

6. To cleanse the stables of Augeas, King in Elis. Augeas owned 3,000 magnificent cattle, none of which ever sickened or died; the stables had not been cleaned in 30 years. With the stipulation that he would receive one-tenth of the cattle for his work, Heracles diverted the rivers Alpheus and Peneus from their beds and washed out the stables in a single day.

7. To bring back from Crete the white bull beloved by Pasiphaë. Declining any help from King Minos, Heracles subdued the animal single-handedly and rode on its back as it swam the seas from Crete to Greece.

8. To capture the wild, flesh-eating mares of Diomedes of Thrace. Heracles slew Diomedes and fed him to his own mares, who thereupon became tame enough to be harnessed to a chariot. The hero then drove them back to Eurystheus, consecrated them to Hera, and set them free on Mount Olympus.

9. To obtain from Hyppolyte, Queen of the Amazons, the girdle given her by her father Ares, god of war. In the land of the Amazons, Heracles was cordially received by Hyppolyte, who readily agreed to give him her girdle. But Hera gave out a rumor that Heracles intended to betray their queen, and the angry Amazons seized arms to attack him. Heracles, believing himself to have been tricked, killed Hyppolyte, evaded the warrior women, and with the girdle made off for Mycenae.

10. To steal the cattle belonging to Geryon, a fearful winged man-monster with three heads (or three bodies), who lived on the island of Erythea west of the Mediterranean. His prized red cattle were guarded day and night by the giant herdsman, Eurytion, and by Orthus, a fierce two-headed dog, brother to Cerberus, guardian of the gateway to Hades. With his club Heracles slew first the herds-

man, then the dog, and finally Geryon himself. He then drove the cattle from the western mouth of the Mediterranean (where he had stopped to set up the Pillars of Hercules on his way to Erythea) back over land and sea to Mycenae.

This should have been the end of the labors, but Eurystheus contended that two of them did not count, since in slaying the Hydra, Heracles had had the help of Iolaus and since the washing of the Augean stables had been done for pay. Two more labors were therefore required.

11. To fetch a branch from the tree of the golden apples, which grew in a garden belonging to Atlas and was guarded by his three daughters, the Hesperides, and a hundred-headed dragon, Ladon. On his way Heracles found and freed Prometheus, who cautioned him not to pluck the fruit himself. Having reached the garden and killed the dragon, Heracles offered to hold up the sky for Atlas while the giant went to break a spray from the tree. The transfer was made, but with the apples in his hand Atlas decided to convey them himself. Heracles pretended to agree, but asked Atlas to relieve him for a moment so that he might adjust his cloak more comfortably. Atlas did so, whereupon Heracles raced off with his prize, leaving the giant once more supporting the heavens.

12. To fetch Cerberus from Hades. This guardian of the underworld had three heads, a serpent's tail, and a mane of serpents' heads. Heracles was given permission to take the dog if he could subdue him without weapons. Ignoring the stings of the serpents, Heracles seized the animal in his mighty grasp and choked him into submission. After exhibiting the dog to Eurystheus, Heracles led him back to the underworld.

Hobson's Choice

In any given situation, the necessity to accept whatever is offered or go without.

> Where to elect there is but one,
> 'Tis Hobson's choice—take that or none.
> —THOMAS WARD, *England's Reformation*, 1638

Although the "choice" in Hobson's choice is mythical, the man who fathered the phrase is not. Tobias Hobson was an English carrier, a small entrepreneur of sorts, who ran his business in such manner as to give rise to the phrase.

Born in Cambridge near the middle of the 16th century, Hobson for 50 years drove a coach carrying passengers, letters, and parcels between the university town and the Bull Inn on Bishopsgate Street in London. As a supplement to his coaching he kept a stable of some 40 horses, together with boots, whips, saddles, and bridles, for hiring out to the students at the various colleges making up Cambridge University. He had one stipulation: whoever came to rent a horse must take the one in the stall next to the door, so that the animals were used in strict rotation. There was no picking or choosing or bargaining of any sort; it was truly Hobson's choice or none.

Hobson's business flourished and his savings grew. He continued to post the 40-odd miles between Cambridge and London, sometimes at reckless speed, until well up in his 80s. Then in the spring of 1630 the plague, which had been harassing England for some years, broke out in the colleges and all classes were suspended. In order to lessen the danger of contamination, Hobson's run was canceled, and the old man found himself bewilderingly at leisure. The ban lasted perhaps six months, being lifted in November; but the shock of a dislocated routine seems to have been too much. Hobson had already taken to his bed and on January 1, 1631, at the age of 86, he died.

His death produced two rhymed epitaphs, memorable in that they were written by one destined to be among the University's most illustrious alumni, John Milton. Although both are written in a humorous vein, there is a touch of kindness in the one entitled "On the University Carrier."

> Here lies old Hobson. Death hath broke his girt,
> And here, alas! hath laid him in the dirt;
> Or else, the ways being foul, twenty to one
> He's here stuck in a slough, and overthrown.
> 'Twas such a shifter, if the truth were known,
> Death was half glad when he had got him down;
> For he had any time this ten years full
> Dodged with him betwixt Cambridge and *The Bull*.
> And surely Death could never have prevailed,
> Had not his weekly course of carriage failed;
> But lately, finding him so long at home,
> And thinking now his journey's end was come,
> And that he had ta'en up his latest Inn,
> In the kind office of a Chamberlin
> Showed him the room where he must lodge the night,
> Pulled off his boots and took away the light.
> If any ask for him, it shall be said,
> "Hobson has supped, and's newly gone to bed."

Hodgkin's Disease

A malignant growth, from obscure causes, of cells in the lymph nodes, spleen, and lymphoid tissues, first described by the English physician Thomas Hodgkin (1798–1866). The disease often begins in the neck and spreads through the body; it is painless but fatal.

Hofmann's Violets

A group of beautiful violet-colored synthetic dyes with a coal-tar base, discovered about 1865 by the German-born chemist August Wilhelm von Hofmann (1818–1892).

The chemical synthesis of dyes is only a little more than a hundred years old, but the art of dyeing woven fabrics in a limited range of colors can be traced back to biblical times.

In those days, dark blue was made from the leaf juice of the indigo plant, clear red from madder roots and the bodies of cochineal insects dried and crushed to a powder, a yellow from saffron (the dried, orange-red stamens of the wild crocus). Ancient Tyre found the secret of purple in sea snails crushed and boiled in a salt solution for three days, hence Tyrian purple. The rarity of this product made it very dear; only the high priests wore "purple and fine linen." Later, kings decreed it a royal hue, forbidding its use by commoners, and a little prince or princess was "born to the purple" in a bed canopied and draped with that luxurious color.

The first substantial change in dyeing methods did not take place until the middle of the 19th century, and that came about quite by accident. In 1845 the Royal College of Science in London decided to institute a first-rate course in chemistry. At the suggestion of Queen Victoria's consort, Prince Albert, the young German chemist August Wilhelm von Hofmann was invited to fill the chair. Hofmann had been experimenting with coal tar, the sticky black substance that forms when coal is heated in a vacuum, and had found that coal tar could be broken down into a number of organic materials, including benzene and the anilines. Pursuing this research while teaching at the Royal College, he eventually took on as assistant an especially bright student, William Henry Perkin, and suggested that the young man try his hand at analyzing coal-tar compounds. Then a chance remark by Hofmann on the possibility of synthesizing quinine turned Perkin's energies to that problem. He didn't solve it, but he did end up with a brilliant purple liquid which he thought might make a useful dye. Further experiments showed not only that he was right but that he had hit upon a method for synthesizing dyes that had a wider color range and were much cheaper than natural dyes.

Justly proud of his pupil's success, Hofmann turned his

own efforts in a similar direction. In 1858 he synthesized a handsome red-purple dye, one of the rosanilines, far superior to madder. The color soon became the rage of French dyers, who patriotically named it magenta in honor of France's victory over Austria at the battle of Magenta the following year. From magenta it was then an easy step to the famous violets, a procedure demonstrated by Hofmann in 1865 shortly after his return to Germany as professor of chemistry at the University of Berlin.

Hooke's Law

The law governing strains within the elastic limit. It states that when a spiral spring is stretched, the amount of stretch is directly proportional to the force applied. The law was discovered in 1676 and published two years later by the English physicist Robert Hooke (1635–1703).

A native of the Isle of Wight, Robert Hooke began his career as a research assistant to Robert Boyle (*see* Boyle's law). From 1662 on he served as curator of experiments to the Royal Society, being elected a Fellow in 1663 and secretary in 1677. His contributions to science ranged over a remarkable number of fields, including mechanics, optics, chemistry, and physiology.

Hooke had been experimenting with the behavior of springs for some years before he came upon the law that bears his name. In order to protect his discovery he announced it first in the form of an anagram: c e i i i n o s s s t t u v. After waiting two years to make sure no one else would lay claim to his idea, he published a translation in 1678: *Ut tensio, sic vis,* that is, "as the stretch, so the force."

Hudson's Bay

One of the world's largest seas (as distinguished from the oceans), 472,000 square miles in area, and lying just below the arctic circle in Canada. The region was explored in 1610 by the English navigator Henry Hudson (d. 1611) in an attempt to find a northwest passage which would be a short cut to the East Indies.

At the time of Hudson's voyages the notion was held that after the first belt of arctic cold had been passed, the climate would grow warmer and the sea lanes would open up. Acting on this surmise, the Muscovy Company, an English joint-stock trading company, in 1607 hired the experienced navigator Henry Hudson to look for a route eastward via the northern polar region.

With ten seamen and his second son, John, Hudson set off on April 19, intending to sail straight across the pole. He got as far as Spitzbergen, but there the ice barrier cut off further passage, and he had to turn back. The following year he tried again, probing the Barents Sea for a northeast opening with as little success. The trip was not a total loss, however, for two of the sailors saw a mermaid, and Hudson carefully recorded their description of her in the logbook.

In 1609, a third expedition was outfitted, this time by the Dutch East India Company. Sailing on the *Half Moon*, the voyagers were approaching Novaya Zemlya, when the crew refused to go further into the cold; and Hudson, knowing that a return to Amsterdam for such reasons would be counted insubordination, persuaded them to turn around and head for the Virginia coast of North America. A map sent him by his friend Captain John Smith indicated a possible passage westward at 40° latitude, approximately where Philadelphia now is; but on cruising along the coast the only likely opening Hudson found was the mouth of the river now called by his name. After 150 miles of sailing upstream, to where Albany is located today, he realized that he would never reach China by this route and started on the return trip to the Netherlands. Putting in at Dartmouth, England, the ship was seized and the English crew members taken off.

A fourth voyage was then promoted by a new, wholly English company. This time there were no digressions. Hudson sailed directly for Davis' "overfall" (now Hudson Strait), which he reached, two months out of London, by the middle of June, 1610. Still moving westward, he finally entered the great bay, concerning which an old map of John Cabot's day comments: "Here a surging sea commences, here [because of proximity to the magnetic pole] ships compasses lose their properties." Hudson was sure he had found the passage at last. For the next months he combed the east shore thoroughly. On October 31, the ship dropped anchor in James Bay and ten days later was frozen in.

The winter passed precariously. A number of the crew fell victim to scurvy, frostbite, and other ills, and rumbles of discontent arose over what seemed to be turning into a fruitless quest. The following spring, shortly after the ice broke, Hudson had a nasty quarrel with one of the men, Henry Greene, over the division of clothing belonging to a seaman who had died.

In retaliation Greene incited a number of others to mutiny, not too difficult under the circumstances. Hudson, his son and seven of the men (including the sick ones), were put adrift in a small boat and abandoned. No trace of them was ever found. Of the mutineers, only a remnant survived the trip home, and those who did were thrown into prison.

Huntington's Chorea

A hereditary disease of the nervous system, characterized by the involuntary muscle twitches observed in

Sydenham's chorea or St. Vitus' dance (*which see*), accompanied by a progressive dementia. It is inevitably fatal. The
disease was described by the American physician George
Huntington (1850–1916).

Huxley's Layer

The middle of three layers making up the inner root
sheath of a hair follicle. It is composed of pigment-bearing
cells of irregular shape, first recognized and demonstrated in
1845 by the eventually famous English biologist Thomas
Henry Huxley (1825–1895), then just graduated from
Charing Cross Hospital. (*See* Darwin's Bulldog.)

Ixion's Wheel

A fiery wheel rolling eternally through the heavens
(or the underworld), to which Zeus ordered Ixion bound,
after discovering that the latter had planned to seduce
Zeus's wife, Hera.

Ixion, son of Phlegyas, King of the Lapiths in Thessaly,
wooed Dia, daughter of Eionius, and promised rich gifts for
Eionius' consent to the marriage. After the wedding, however, Ixion had second thoughts and resolved not to honor
his pledge. He had a deep pit dug in front of the palace,
lined with live coals and cunningly concealed. When
Eionius came to receive the gifts, he tumbled into the pit
and was burned to death.

For this treacherous deed Ixion found himself an outcast.
No one would speak to him, nor could he find anyone who
would purify him of his crime. Finally Zeus, looking down
from Olympus, took pity on the wanderer, performed the
ritual himself, and even brought the unhappy man to dine
at the table of the gods.

Ixion repaid this kindness with the basest ingratitude.
Struck by the beauty and grace of Hera, he determined to

have her for his own. Zeus read his thoughts and caused a cloud to assume the shape and features of Hera, so that it was Nephele the cloud instead of the queen of the gods whom Ixion embraced (and who later bore a son Centaurus, pregenitor of the centaurs). For this insolence and attempted betrayal Zeus had Hermes bind Ixion hand and foot to the wheel of fire and condemned him to revolve in agony forever.

Ixion, whom Greek mythology records as the first murderer, suffers eternal punishment only for his crime against the gods; the crime against his fellow man is considered expiable through the rite of purification. The obligation to beg for absolution is embodied in his very name: *Ixion* means comer or suppliant, from the verb *ikein,* to come.

Jablochkoff's Candles

An improved form of arc light, invented in 1876 by the Russian electrical engineer Paul Jablochkoff (1847–1894).

When two carbon rods are mounted a small distance apart and an electric current is applied, a continuous spark passes from the tip of one rod to that of the other. This is the principle of the arc light. The earliest lights, however, flickered badly because the carbon rods burned down unevenly, and mechanical attempts to regulate the process were complicated and expensive.

Jablochkoff's "candles," a refinement of the apparatus, were an answer to the problem. He joined the vertically set rods at the top with a small crosspiece, also of carbon, and placed between them a strip of porcelain clay which vaporized as the lamp burned. When electric current was applied, the carbon crosspiece was rapidly consumed and an arc of light was formed between the tips of the uprights. Alternating current was used, replacing the customary direct current, so that the rods would burn evenly and thus reduce flickering to a minimum. Four such pairs of rods, in a later development, set four-square and enclosed in a glass globe, gave a satisfactory, long-lasting illumination.

Jacob's Coat

(Jacob's membrane). The bacillary layer of the retina, so called because it contains the rodlike parts of the photoreceptors, the light-and-color-perceiving rods and cones (Latin *bacillus*, rod). It was discovered and described in 1819 by the Irish ocular pathologist Arthur Jacob (1790–1874).

Jacob's Ladder

A ship's ladder of rope or chain with wooden or iron rungs, used for climbing from the deck to the rigging, or a European (and related American) perennial herb of the phlox family which bears bright blue or white flowers and has a stalk whose twin leaves branch horizontally at regular intervals along the stem like the rungs of a ladder. In the biblical story, Jacob, son of Isaac, dreamt of a ladder stretching from earth to heaven and filled with angels coming and going. At the top the Lord Himself sat in great glory, blessing Jacob and his descendants, who were to be in numbers "like the dust of the earth" (Genesis 28). (*See also* Jacob's Pillow.)

Jacob's Pillow

The stone that Jacob used for a pillow the night he dreamed of a ladder reaching from earth to heaven, with "the angels of God ascending and descending" (Genesis 28). Jacob had been fleeing from the wrath of his brother Esau, whom he had tricked out of their father's blessing, when, overtaken by darkness, he lay down in an open

field to sleep. On awakening, awed by the vision of divine
glory, he took the stone on which he had slept and set it on
end to mark the holy place, which he called Bethel, or
House of God. (*See also* Jacob's Ladder.)

Jacob's Staff

(*Baculus Jacobi*). An improvement on the cross-
staff, a navigational instrument for taking the elevation of
the sun or a star or for measuring the angular distance
between two stars. The device was introduced in 1342 by
the Jewish mathematician, astronomer, philosopher, and
biblical commentator, Levi ben Gerson (1288–*c*. 1344) of
Montpellier, France.

The cross-staff, it appears, was invented in the 13th century by one Jacob ben Mahir and comprised a rod of wood
or metal furnished with a sliding crosspiece set at right
angles. With one end of the rod held close to the eye, the
crosspiece was moved forward or backward until its lower
tip was even with the horizon and its upper tip just covered
the star or the sun. Then the angle formed by the rod and
a line from eyepoint to the horizon, multiplied by two, gave
the elevation of the heavenly body.

Levi ben Gerson (Gersonides) improved the device by
adding a diagonal, graduated scale to the staff, from which
the angle of elevation could easily be read off. Sailors
called Jacob's staff the *balestilha* (from balestier or cross-
bowman), since they aimed it like an ancient crossbow in
order to "shoot" the sun and stars.

The name Jacob's staff has also been applied to a pil-
grim's staff (this use is now obsolete). It can also refer to a
walking stick concealing a sword or dagger and a plant, the
Great mullein or Aaron's rod (*which see*).

Jacob's Stone

The stone on which the kings of Scotland, from the 9th century to the 13th, knelt to receive their crowns; also called stone of destiny or stone of Scone. According to legend it was the actual stone that served as a pillow for the biblical Jacob when he had his dream of the ladder and the angels (*see* Jacob's Ladder and Jacob's Pillow). A more reliable historical account states that after Kenneth Mac-Alpine became king of the Picts and Scots in 844 A.D., he brought the stone of destiny from Dunstaffnage to his capital at Scone. Here it remained until 1296, when Edward I of England defeated the Scots under John Balliol, took the stone away, and placed it under the coronation throne in Westminster Abbey. It is still there, despite some agitation that it be returned to the Scots as a "generous gesture."

Jacob's Well

The town well in the city of Samaria called Sychar in biblical days, now Nablus, near the field that Jacob gave to his son Joseph. Here Jesus asked a "woman of Samaria" for a drink, and she, greatly surprised, replied, "How is it that you, a Jew, ask a drink of me, a woman of Samaria?" For, the Bible goes on, Jews have no dealings with Samaritans (John 4:5–9).

Jacobs' Cavern

A cave in Pineville, McDonald County, in the extreme southwest corner of Missouri. It was minutely explored in 1903 by the Arkansas archeologist, E. H. Jacobs, and two colleagues and is of scientific interest because of the discovery of 6 human skeletons, the bones of 12 different kinds of animals, and a rich collection of flint knives and stone artifacts. The absence of fine pottery marks the occupants as an earlier people than the mound builders. The civilization dates from around the beginning of the Christian era.

Jacobson's Organ

A chemoreceptor, that is, an organ sensitive to chemical stimuli arising from food or odors, part of the olfactory system of most vertebrates. It was described in 1811 by the Danish anatomist Ludwig Levin (Louis) Jacobson (1783–1843).

Jamie Keddie's Ring

A ring possessing the magic power of making its wearer invisible, said to have been found long ago by the tailor Jamie Keddie in a cavern of the Hill of Kinnoull that rises just across the river from Perth, Scotland. It is referred to in Sir Walter Scott's *The Fair Maid of Perth,* where Catherine's father, Simon Glover, teases his daughter about trying to slip out unseen to meet the young man she was in love with. "What," says Simon, "thou thoughtst thou hadst Jamie Keddie's ring, and couldst walk invisible?"

Jenkins' Ear

(War of). A war between England and Spain that broke out in October, 1739, brought on by a Spanish outrage against the British sloop-master Robert Jenkins but having its roots in Spain's attempt to curtail England's freedom of trade.

By the Treaty of Utrecht (1713), Spain and England reached an agreement whereby England was allowed limited trade with Spanish America. But English privateers used this foot in the door to press for wider access to South America, with the result that incidents of smuggling and searches for contraband began to pile up.

One such episode in 1731 had an unforeseen and far-reaching effect. The Scottish merchant ship *Rebecca,* out of Jamaica for England, was halted by a Spanish *guarda costa,* boarded, and searched thoroughly. No illegal cargo was found; nevertheless, as its captain, Robert Jenkins, reported later, the Spanish officer had abused and maltreated him, had torn off one of his ears, and then told him to carry it back to his king with the word that if His Majesty had been in Jenkins' shoes he would have received the same treatment.

Jenkins took his ear and the message back to George II, who seems to have given little attention to either at the time. By 1738, however, relations with Spain were worsening. Someone remembered the Jenkins incident, and a bar committee of the House of Commons was set up to inquire further into his story. This time the ship captain was listened to with more interest. His bearing and his account made quite an impression, especially when, asked what he had done in that hour of peril, he replied: "I recommended my soul to God and my cause to my country."

The maltreatment of so sturdy a patriot, Dr. Tobias Smollett records in his *Compleat History of England* (1811), "filled the whole house with indignation," an indignation soon transformed into a public demand for satisfaction. The limiting clauses of the Spanish trade treaty had never sat well with the British, and the Jenkins affair was one straw too many. The sober voice of Prime Minister Robert Walpole was drowned out, and within a year England declared war on Spain.

Historians of a later date have tended to view the incident with less emotion and some with outright skepticism. "It is certain," wrote Lord Mahon in his own *History of England* (1858), "that Jenkins had lost an ear, or part of an ear, which he always carried about with him wrapped in cotton, to display to his audience; but I find it alleged by no mean authority, that he had lost it on another occasion, and perhaps, as seems to be insinuated, in the pillory."

Jephthah's Daughter

The only child of the Gileadite Jephthah (later one of the judges in Israel), sacrificed by her father to fulfill a vow that if he were successful in battle he would offer up the first living thing that came to meet him after the victory.

A son of Gilead by a harlot, Jephthah had been driven from home and land and had become a leader of a band of raiders. When the Ammonites threatened to invade Israel, however, the elders came seeking him to defend them against the enemy. Jephthah agreed, on condition that he was to become chief if he won, and a solemn compact was entered into. Jephthah then took his vow that in return for victory he would make a burnt offering of "whomsoever comes forth from the doors of my house."

The word "whomsoever" suggests that Jephthah was not ruling out the possibility of a human sacrifice (a custom occasionally practiced, although frowned upon by prophets and teachers). But that it might be his dear and only child, who came so joyfully to greet him with timbrels and dancing, had not occurred to him; and he could only cry out in agony, "Alas, my daughter, you have brought me very low!" But to the young girl—we do not even know her name—as to her father, a vow was inviolable, and she nobly and courageously resigned herself to its fulfillment.

"And it became the custom in Israel that the daughters of Israel went year by year to lament the daughter of Jephthah the Gileadite four days in the year" (Judges 11:40).

Job's Comforters

A term for those who come apparently to commiserate and console in time of trouble, but who instead either find fault, utter truisms, or offer words that are cold and empty. It refers to the three men who visited the biblical Job in the time of his affliction.

Job's misfortunes were sent to test his sincerity and devotion to God. Wealthy and the head of a happy family, he was, as the Lord of Heaven boasted to Satan, "a blameless and upright man." Satan replied that it was easy for one so blessed with possessions to praise the Giver, but if he were stripped of them would he still be faithful? "Behold, he is in your power; only spare his life," said the Lord. In the misfortunes that followed, Job lost all of his sons and daughters, his servants, his flocks and herds, and he himself was covered with loathsome boils.

"Then he took a potsherd with which to scrape himself, and sat among the ashes," says the Bible. Here he was found by his three friends, Eliphaz the Temanite, Bildad the Shuhite, and Zophar the Naamathite. They were shocked at the miserable state to which their friend had been reduced, and felt it their duty to search out the reasons why a man who had always led so exemplary a life should have been so ill treated.

In the ensuing discussion, cast in the form of a poem, each of the friends pursues the question according to his lights. Eliphaz, who came from the land of Edom, famous for its wise men, lays out the problem with seemingly impeccable logic. Since prosperity is the reward for righteousness and adversity is the penalty of sin, the fact that Job is suffering proves that he *must* have sinned, whether he is aware of it or not. Bildad, on the other hand, is the purveyor of commonplaces and homely sayings. God is all righteous and all just; He properly punishes sinners; if Job is indeed upright his prayers will not go unanswered—words so wide of the mark that Job impatiently brushes them away. Lastly Zophar reveals the unfeeling objectivity of the fatalist, which runs through much of the Wisdom literature of which the Book of Job is a part. There is no point in man's attempting to search out evil, says Zophar. God can see evil where even the best of men cannot, and the punishment He metes out is less than the guilty deserve. The only wisdom, then, is blind obedience.

But none of these explanations satisfies Job. Turning from man to God, he flings the question up to Heaven: What has he done in his long life to merit such treatment? Thereupon a great whirlwind arises. Speaking "out of the whirlwind," the Almighty delivers a majestic recital of the wonders of nature and the powers of the Most High, and Job, overwhelmed by the revelation of such glory, humbly acknowledges that he can only despise himself and "repent in dust and ashes." Yet the Lord also knows that Job, in spite of his tribulations and though urged by his wife to "curse God and die," has never departed from his faith. Heaven has triumphed over Satan, and Job's fortunes are restored twice over.

As for the "comforters," God's wrath was kindled against them, for they "had not spoken of me what is right, as my servant Job has." Therefore they must make an expiatory sacrifice, which God will accept only after Job has prayed that He do so.

Job's Tears

A species of Asiatic grass, *Maydaea,* that also includes maize or Indian corn. The tear-shaped seeds are enclosed in a hard covering, which is blue-white when ripe, and are used as beads.

Jonson's Learnéd Sock

An allusion by John Milton to a Ben Jonson comedy. The "sock" was a light shoe worn by actors in Greek and Roman comedies; by extension it came to mean comic drama. The phrase is from Milton's "L'Allegro," where the poet is describing the delightful pleasures, including the theater, found in cities, and invites us

> Then to the well-trod stage anon
> If Jonson's learnéd sock be on,
> Or sweetest Shakespeare, Fancy's child,
> Warbling his native wood-notes wild.

Joseph's Coat

A sleeved robe reaching to the ground (the "coat of many colors") made by Jacob for "the son of his old age," his favorite, Joseph (Genesis 37). The ordinary tunic was knee length and sleeveless, and the longer garment was a mark of special favor. The term also refers to a showy annual, *Amaranthus tricolor,* growing 2 to 4 feet high, with richly variegated leaves.

Kepler's Dream

A treatise in the form of a fable written by the astronomer Johannes Kepler (1571–1630) and published posthumously, describing how the movements of the heavenly bodies would look to an inhabitant of the moon and including a "moon geography."

When Johannes Kepler was admitted to the University of Tübingen in 1589 as a student of theology, one of his teachers was Magister Michael Maestlin, professor of mathematics and astronomy. Although the rest of the faculty, citing holy writ, held with Ptolemy that the universe revolves around the earth, Maestlin was a confirmed believer in the heliocentric theory announced less than a half century earlier by Copernicus. In his public lectures, Maestlin taught Ptolemy, but to a select and intimate circle, of which young Kepler was one, he expounded on the structure of the universe as Copernicus had laid it out.

Later, Kepler began to jot down some thoughts as to how
the motions of the stars and planets including the earth
would look to someone living on the moon. For a time
these thoughts remained notes only, but his interest was
revived when he encountered Plutarch's *On the Face of
the Moon's Disc*. The idea then began to take shape of
writing a detailed description of the moon in fanciful form.
In the summer of 1609, when he was living in Prague
under appointment as imperial mathematician, he discussed his plan with a learned friend, Wackher von Wack-
enfels, and thereupon sat down and composed his *Somnium
seu Astronomia Lunari*—a *Dream or Astronomy of the
Moon*.

The end product was a remarkable blend of scientific
fact and imaginative fantasy. In it Kepler dreams of himself as a youth living in Thule with his mother, a gentle
soul conversant with wise and friendly spirits who often
convey her to distant lands or bring her news of other far
places. One such place is Levania. In the course of describing the inhabitants, plants, and animals of this imaginary land, Kepler sets down the actual results of his
own many years of astronomical observations. In contrast to
the fanciful "geography" drawn from Plutarch, Kepler pre-
sents with great accuracy the phenomena exhibited by the
sun, the earth, and the other planets as they would appear
from the moon. These include the alternation of day and
night, heat and cold and the seasons, and the paths of the
planets. It was Kepler who first determined that the planetary orbits were elliptical rather than circular. All this, as
he put it, was "to make an argument for the motion of the
earth taking the moon as an example." To the body of the
work he later added numerous notes, astronomical, physical
and geographic, which greatly enhanced its scientific value;
and he finished it off with his own Latin translation from
the Greek of Plutarch's "moon geography."

Although the *Dream* was not published during Kepler's lifetime, a number of sketches of it were made which passed from hand to hand among astronomers and other scientists and intellectuals, who found it provocative and exciting. No one, therefore, was prepared for a turn of events which caused the document to have near fatal consequences.

Witchhunting reached a peak in Germany in the early 1600s. In the spring of 1615 one of those accused was Kepler's mother, then living in Leonberg in the duchy of Württemberg.

Kepler, who was working as court mathematician in Linz, heard nothing of this until almost the end of the year. He at once dispatched a furious letter to the councillor of Leonberg, lashing out at the attempt to persecute and bring to the rack a defenseless old woman and stating his intention of fighting all charges until they were wiped out.

The letter put a stop to whispered accusations against Kepler, but it had no effect on the court action against his mother, an action which dragged on for the next five years.

A hearing was finally held in May, 1618. The proceedings continued sporadically for two more years, while a case of witchcraft was constructed out of the most fantastic testimony, from some 30 or 40 witnesses. In July, 1620, the order went out to arrest "the Kepler woman" and if she did not confess, to bring her to torture.

Kepler in Linz was informed of the crisis by his sister Margarete. He immediately wrote to the Duke of Württemberg, declaring that, since he was eternally obligated to his mother by divine and natural rights, he would attend the trial and take an active part in the proceedings himself. This he did, even to writing most of the concluding statement.

His mother continued her sturdy defiance both during the trial and after she was returned to prison. Loaded with chains, brought into the torture chamber itself and made to look upon the horrible instruments, she still did not break. "Do with me what you will," she declared. "I have nothing to admit."

Finally, the Duke decreed that the terror Frau Kepler had undergone during her 14 months imprisonment had invalidated the "evidence," and on October 4, 1621, she was released.

King Alfred's Cakes

A batch of oaten cakes put to bake by a swineherd's wife and left in the care of the fugitive Alfred the Great (848?–899), who let them burn because, absorbed in thought, he forgot to turn them.

Though probably no more than a tale, the story of King Alfred's cakes has some basis in historical fact. The fifth son of King Athelwulf, Alfred had become King of Wessex in 871. That year the Danes were driven off to other parts of England, and Alfred's kingdom was at peace; but five years later hostilities broke out again in the south, and by early spring of 878 Alfred and a small band had been forced into hiding at Athelney. They stayed for several months until plans for a renewed assault were completed, then with augmented forces moved against the Danes and beat them decisively.

It is during the Athelney period that the episode of the cakes supposedly occurred. First appearing in print in 1574, it is one of a number of "interpolations" by Archbishop Matthew Parker into a life of Alfred, written by the Welsh bishop John Asser, probably in 893. The only known manuscript of Asser's *Annales rerum gestarum Alfredi magni,* dating from the year 1000, was destroyed by fire in 1731, so that Parker's interpolated version is all that scholars have to go on. Careful research has winnowed out Parker's embellishments from the chronicle as set down out of Asser's

personal knowledge; and the current scrupulously anno-
tated text by W. H. Stevenson, the English scholar, has
Parker conveniently bracketed off. Stevenson says there is
no evidence that the story of Alfred and the cakes even
existed before the Norman Conquest, two centuries after
Alfred's time. Then it is found in various versions including
a 12th-century one in which the King obeyed the swineherd
(not the wife) and managed to turn the cakes in time.

For those who may want to try Parker's straightforward
Latin, here it is:

"Contigit autem die quodam, ut rustica, uxor videlicet
illius vaccarii, pararet ad coquendum panes, et ille rex
sedens sic circa focum praeparavit sibi arcum et sagittas
et alia bellorum instrumenta. Cum vero panes ad ignem
positos ardentes aspexit illia infelix mulier, festinanter
(cu)currit et amovit eos, increpans regem invictissimum, et
dicens:

> Heus homo
> urere, quos cernis, panes gyrare moraris
> cum nimium gaudes hos manducare calentes!

Mulier illa infausta minime putabat illium esse regem
AElfredum, qui tot bella gessit contra paganos, tantasque
victorias accepit de eis."

King Solomon's Ring

A magic ring worn by Solomon, which enabled him
to understand the speech of birds and beasts, and gave him
power over all living things, all the forces of nature, and
the unseen world of the supernatural.

The story of how the great king acquired his ring comes
out of Moslem tradition. After Solomon had buried his
father, David, in the ancestral tomb, he started back to
Jerusalem. In a little dale between Hebron and the holy

city he sat down to rest, fell asleep, and had a most wonderful dream.

There came to him eight angels, rulers of the eight winds, of marvelous bearing. Of these the greatest addressed himself to Solomon and gave him a jewel inscribed "God is Power and Greatness," with which the King would have command over all the winds of heaven.

Then there came four angels, one in the likeness of a whale, one like an eagle, one like a lion, and one like a serpent. The angel like an eagle gave Solomon a jewel inscribed "Let all creatures praise the Lord!" so that he might rule over all the creatures of the earth.

Then came a mighty angel whose upper half was like the earth and whose lower half was like the waters. The stone he gave bore the words "Heaven and earth serve God," and with it Solomon would have dominion over land and sea.

The angel also gave Solomon still another gem, on which was written "There is no God but God and Mohammed is the messenger of God," and now Solomon had power over the Jinns, the Afreets, and all the world of spirits.

Solomon awoke, and beside him were the jewels. When he returned home he had the stones placed in a ring, which he wore ever after, and ruled wisely over his land.

Leeuwenhoek's Little Animals

A darting swarm of protozoa—one-celled organisms —discovered during the summer of 1674 by the Dutch microscopist Anthony van Leeuwenhoek (1632–1723) when he examined a drop of pond water with the high-powered lens he had invented.

Anthony van Leeuwenhoek had been a linen merchant in Delft before he became interested in the construction and use of microscopes. Finding the compound instruments then employed less effective than a single lens, he began to grind his own glass. The result was a short-focus, very powerful lens, which he kept a secret. All sorts of materials came under his microscope, and he reported his findings regularly to the Royal Society of London.

That the sluggish-seeming pond water should be so bustlingly alive surprised and delighted him, and he wrote graphically of his "little animals" in a letter of September 7, 1674:

> These animalcules had divers colors, some being whitish, others pellucid; others had green and very shining little scales, others again were green in the middle, and before and behind white, others greyish. And the motion of most of them in the water was so swift, and so various upwards, downwards and round about, that I confess I could not but wonder at it.

By his investigations into the life cycles of various minute forms of life, Leeuwenhoek made a number of contributions toward disproving the doctrine of spontaneous generation, then beginning to be questioned. He showed, among other things, that weevils are not "bred" from wheat, but are grubs hatched from eggs laid in the grain by winged insects, and that shellfish and fleas are not generated out of sand, nor eels from dew.

Lot's Wife

The unhappy spouse of Abraham's nephew, who, while fleeing from the predicted destruction of Sodom and Gomorrah, and against heavenly admonition, looked back regretfully at the wicked cities and was turned into a pillar of salt (Genesis 19).

Lot and Abraham, with their large and growing households, had come up together from Egypt to Bethel. To avoid conflict, Abraham proposed that they move into separate areas and gave Lot the choice: "If you take the left hand, I will go to the right; if you take the right hand, I will go to the left." Lot saw that the valley of the Jordan, peopled with the inhabitants of the two thriving cities, Sodom and Gomorrah, was fair and fertile. He took his way there, leaving his uncle on the bare hills of Bethel above Canaan.

Though living near the cities of sin, Lot seems not to have been ensnared by them, so that when God determined to destroy them He made provision for Lot to be saved.

Lot as well as his wife showed a reluctance to leave. When the angels urged them to hurry to the safety of the distant hills, Lot wheedled another compromise out of the Deity— to be allowed to go to the city of Zoar. This dispensation also granted, the party finally moved off, but Lot's wife, who some say was named Edith, lingered and looked back.

At the southwest end of the Dead Sea there is a curious formation called *Jebel Usdum,* "the mountain of Sodom," a range of cliffs perhaps 6 miles long and 600 feet high, of crystallized rock salt capped with chalky limestone and gypsum. Under a beating rain the salt washes away in deep perpendicular furrows, with segments of the cliff sometimes becoming completely detached. One segment towering 40 feet and set on a kind of pedestal that raises it still higher above the Dead Sea, appears very like the figure of a woman and today is called "Lot's Wife."

Luther's 95 Theses

A document attacking many medieval practices of the Catholic Church, including the custom of selling indulgences and the doctrinal basis for granting them. The theses were supposedly nailed to the door of the Castle Church at Wittenberg on October 31, 1517, by the German theologian and Augustinian monk Martin Luther (1483–1546), who later became a leader of the Reformation.

Indulgences are defined in Catholic doctrine as "the remission before God of the temporal punishment due to sin after the guilt has been forgiven." Authority for the Church to grant indulgences was derived from appropriate passages in Matthew and John. In the solemn Jubilee years, proclaimed by various popes, the number of indulgences made available was greatly increased.

During the Middle Ages the practice grew up of obtaining these remissions through money contributions as an earnest of repentance. The funds thus collected went to the support, adornment, and further construction of a multitude of churches.

As time went on, a number of abuses crept in. In 1515 a two-year Jubilee was declared, the money to go toward the rebuilding of St. Peter's in Rome. By that time, trafficking in indulgences had in many places become a flourishing business. Luther, then engaged in lecturing and preaching in Wittenberg, was spurred into action when a Dominican monk named Johann Tetzel set up shop in Jüterborg a few miles away, selling sealed letters of credit for sins not yet committed.

Luther drew up a series of charges, the 95 theses, which he is reported to have nailed up on the church door. He also sent a copy to the archbishop.

Within the last decade German church historians have asked whether Luther actually posted his theses with hammer and nails? Those who argue the negative say that Luther himself never mentioned the incident in any of his writings. Those who affirm the fact point to indirect, internal evidence.

MacFarlane's Lantern

A popular Scottish name for the moon. According to Sir Walter Scott (1771–1832) the clan of MacFarlane, living on the mountainous slopes above Loch Lomond, was notorious for raiding the lowlands and making off with cattle and other livestock. Since the clan members usually moved by night, the moon came to be called their lantern.

Macgillicuddy's Reeks

A mountain range towering over beautiful Lake Killarney in County Kerry, southwest Ireland.

Reeks is Middle English for ricks, such as hay ricks or stacks. Macgillicuddy's highest peak is Carrantuohill, which rises 3,414 feet into the blue sky.

Martha's Vineyard

(Martin's Vineyard). A triangular-shaped island some 5 miles off the southwest coast of Massachusetts, believed to have been first discovered by Leif Ericsson in the early 11th century. It was not settled, however, until the middle of the 17th century and is now a popular summer resort and artist's haven.

For many years a center for the whaling and fishing industries of New England, the 100 square miles of Martha's Vineyard is set in the midst of strong tides and swirling currents. The Norse discoverers had named it Straumey, "Island of Currents," while to the Indians it was Noë-pe, "Amid the Waters."

The son of Eric the Red left no settlement, being content with exploring the new land and gathering specimens of wheat, vines, and what he called *mösur* wood to take back to Iceland. Half a millennium later, in 1524, Giovanni da Verrazano, sailing up the North American coast from what is now North Carolina, visited the island briefly and recorded it as Luisa. In 1602 the English navigator Bartholomew Gosnold, in a ship chartered by Sir Walter Raleigh, made the island one of his New World stops. His chief interest was the sassafras he found there. He or some member of his crew noted down the island as Martin's Vineyard. Four years later Samuel de Champlain, sighting its picturesque hills while on a cruise of exploration from Canada, logged it as La Soupçonneuse, "Suspicious" or "Doubtful," not being sure whether it was an island or part of the Massachusetts coast. Finally, in 1642, Thomas Mayhew, a merchant of Watertown, England, sent out a company to found a settlement, and Great Harbour, now Edgartown, was established.

The name Martha may have been applied not to the Vineyard but to a smaller island sighted by the Gosnold expedition and lying to the southwest, now called Noman's Land after an Indian named Tequenoman. The place was referred to as Martin's Vineyard until about 1700, and then by some unknown process took on the name of its little neighbor.

Mary's Little Lamb

The precocious animal that followed her young mistress to school and was immortalized some years later in what is now a classic set of nursery verses.

At the time she wrote the verse (1829) Mrs. Sarah Josepha Hale, then living in Boston, was the editor of *Ladies' Magazine*, which was later merged with *Godey's Lady's Book* (*which see*). A composer of sorts, Lowell Mason, had asked her for some suitable lyrics for children to sing in school, and she obliged with "Mary Had a Little Lamb." The following year the jingles were included in a 24-page paperback pamphlet, *Poems For Our Children*, which enjoyed an agreeable popularity for some years thereafter.

A half century later the Old South Church of Boston, famous for having harbored the rally that led to the Boston

Tea Party, was threatened with being torn down because of a lack of funds to keep it in repair. A campaign was launched to save the building, and one of those who responded to the appeal was Mrs. Mary E. (Sawyer) Tyler. Unraveling a pair of stockings knitted from the first fleece shorn, she said, from "Mary's lamb," she cut the wool into short strands, tied these into little bundles with ribbon, fastened the bundles to cards, and sold them at ten cents apiece for the benefit of the church. The story accompanying the cards was that as a youngster Mrs. Tyler did have a pet lamb, and that one day it trotted along with her to the schoolhouse at Redstone Hill. This was in 1817, when she was about 11 years old. A chance observer of the unusual procession was a young man named John Roulstone who, Mrs. Tyler claimed, then dashed off the three famous quatrains.

While the ownership of the lamb seems never to have been disputed, the Roulstone authorship of the commemorative lines was always vigorously denied. Indeed, there is a letter from Mrs. Hale, dated December 29, 1875, which says flatly, "I wrote the original song of 'Mary's Lamb' in 1829 in Boston." Nonetheless, when Henry Ford bought the Redstone Hill schoolhouse in 1926 to preserve it as a landmark, the memorial plaque named Roulstone as the author of the first twelve lines of the poem and Sarah Hale as having added twelve more to complete it.

Maxwell's Demon

A tiny imaginary creature used in 1866 by the Scottish physicist James Clerk Maxwell (1831–1879) to illustrate how it is theoretically possible to thwart the second law of thermodynamics (the name *demon* being first applied by Lord Kelvin in 1867).

Thermodynamics is a branch of physics that deals with

the phenomenon of heat as a form of energy. The first law of thermodynamics, known as the law of the conservation of energy, states that while energy can be transformed, it cannot be either created or destroyed.

The second law may be formulated as follows: When two bodies of unequal temperature are brought into contact, heat energy will flow spontaneously from the hot body to the cold one until the temperatures are equal, but it will not flow in the opposite direction without the application of outside energy. For example, a cup of tea will cool of itself to room temperature, but the heat that has been lost from the tea into the air will not flow from the air back into the tea. To heat the tea again it must be put on the fire.

Maxwell began his experiments in thermodynamics at a time when scientists had come to identify heat with the motion of molecules—the more rapid the motion the greater the heat. The simpler properties of gases were known best and attention was centered on the gas molecule.

In reflecting on the phenomena of heat, Maxwell hit upon a "thought experiment" to illustrate the underlying laws. He reasoned that the molecules in motion in a given volume of gas at a given temperature (temperature being measured by the *average* molecular velocity) would occasionally collide with one another, and when this happened one molecule would gain energy (move faster, become "hotter") while the other would lose energy (move more slowly, "cool" slightly). Since the *amount* of heat energy thus lost and gained was the same, the *temperature* of the gas would remain constant.

Maxwell then considered an insulated vessel full of air at a uniform temperature, with some of its molecules moving with varying velocities. He supposed the vessel to be separated into two parts, A and B, by a partition containing a very small hole fitted with a frictionless shutter and of a size to permit just one molecule at a time to pass through.

He further supposed that there was a little creature in the vessel with eyesight keen enough to see the individual molecules moving about. As a faster-moving molecule in part B approached the partition, the creature would open the shutter to permit the molecule to enter part A. When a slower-moving molecule in A neared the opening, it would be admitted into B. In this way all the hotter, faster molecules would eventually find themselves in A and all the cooler, slower ones in B.

The result would be that the air in B would have cooled, and the air in A would have become heated. A temperature difference would have been produced *without resort to any outside source of energy,* and the second law of thermodynamics would be upset!

McGuffey's Readers

A series of six graded elementary school readers and a speller, written by William Holmes McGuffey of Oxford, Ohio (1800–1873), and his brother, Alexander, intended particularly for children in the rural and backwoods areas of the United States.

During the 21 years between 1836 and 1857, there appeared in the little rustic schools of the South and West a series of books that introduced an entirely new element into the teaching of reading. Until that time use of the *New England Primer* was the approved method of initiating young minds into the mysteries of the alphabet. The *Primer* was sparsely illustrated and contained a text as gloomy as its entry for A: "In Adam's fall/We sinnéd all."

McGuffey's Readers, on the other hand, dealt with the down-to-earth subjects of daily living. They had attractive green covers and pictures on every page. Well-known animals in their natural habitat were generously scattered through the text, and boys and girls were drawn and described in recognizable, familiar situations in field, farm, and woods. In McGuffey's, A was for Ax.

The notion for such a series did not originate with the author, but with a Cincinnati printer named Winthrop Smith. He first broached his plan to Catherine Beecher, who, with her sister Harriet, was running a girls' school in Cincinnati. Catherine suggested that Smith get in touch with a William H. McGuffey, professor of languages at Miami University in Oxford, Ohio, and an ordained Presbyterian minister.

McGuffey was more than happy to accept the offer. His own schooling had been acquired under great difficulties. Books were hard to come by, and he had had to memorize long passages from those lent him by a sympathetic teacher. Prior to settling down at Miami University he had ridden circuit as a roving teacher in Ohio, Western Pennsylvania, and Kentucky, and he had very definite ideas on how to hold the interest of and teach the youngsters of the small towns, plains, and hill country.

His aim was to lay a solid foundation for correct spelling, pronunciation, and usage. At the same time his text, while dealing with the everyday life of immigrant, farm, and pioneer families, stressed character building through useful work and a respect for learning. By providing material suitable for all tastes and ages, McGuffey hoped to encourage parents to study along with their sons and daughters.

The *First* and *Second Readers,* the *First* with an illustrated alphabet, came out in 1836 and were an instant success. The following year two more appeared, the *Third* containing short stories, the *Fourth* made up of lessons in natural history and physics. Alexander's speller was published in 1844, and his *Rhetorical Guide* of the same year was later expanded into two, the *Fifth* and *Sixth Advanced Readers.*

McGuffey seems to have been a much better teacher than

businessman, or perhaps Smith was a better businessman than printer. The contract between the two guaranteed a 10 percent royalty on all copies sold until the copyright sum of 1,000 dollars was reached, after which the *Readers* became the absolute property of the publisher. By the early 1900s, when they were finally replaced by more modern textbooks, McGuffey's *Readers* had sold 122 million copies.

Mendeléyev's Table

A periodic chart of the chemical elements arranged in order of their atomic weights and within that order divided into 8 periods, the end of each period being marked by one of the noble (inert) gases. It was developed in partial form and published in March, 1869, by the Russian chemist Dmitri I. Mendeléyev (1834–1907). Later many others added to it, often on the basis of predictions derived from the table.

Mill's Canons

Five methods (a canon is a method) of discovering and demonstrating cause-effect relationships set out by the English philosopher John Stuart Mill (1806–1873) in his widely read *System of Logic,* first published in 1843.

John Stuart Mill, whose father taught him Greek at the age of three and Latin when he was eight, grew up to become one of the most influential of the 19th-century philosophers. Schooled in history, logic, mathematics, and political economy, social and political philosophy, and ethics, his most notable contributions were to the disciplines of methodology and inductive logic.

The methods of experimental inquiry proposed by Mill were designed to locate the probable cause for an occurrence or effect. "The simplest and most obvious" procedure, he wrote in Chapter VIII of the *Logic,* is really twofold. The first, the method of agreement, states that if a certain phenomenon (effect) is present in a number of instances that differ in all respects save one, then the one respect in which they all *agree* is the cause of the phenomenon. For example, if three diners order three meals all different except that each includes fruit salad, and all three diners get ptomaine poisoning, we may conclude that the fruit salad made them sick.

The second Mills calls the method of difference. Here, if a certain phenomenon is present in one instance and absent in another, and if the two instances agree in all respects save one, then the one respect in which they *differ* is the cause of the phenomenon. As an example, all three diners eat the same meal but one adds fruit salad and only he gets sick, thus we may again conclude that the fruit salad was at fault.

The third is the joint method of agreement and difference, and the fourth, the method of residues. These methods are merely more complicated ways of employing the first two and do not involve any new principle.

The fifth, the method of concomitant variation, states that if a factor varies through a number of instances, and the effect varies as does the factor, that factor is the probable cause of the effect. Thus if one person eats part of his salad and only feels a little ill, the second eats it all and gets sick, while the third eats a double portion and gets very sick, we may safely conclude that the more salad eaten, the more unpleasant will be the result.

The canons have been criticized on the ground that they oversimplify the procedures of scientific inquiry and gloss over the problem of analyzing complex situations into factors.

Mohs's Scale

A set of ten common minerals arranged from very soft to very hard, used in testing the relative hardness of substances by noting whether they scratch or are scratched by one of the known minerals.

One of the founders of modern mineralogy, Friedrich Mohs (1773–1839) was born at Gernrode in the Harz Mountains. It was expected that he would follow in the footsteps of his merchant father, but a strong penchant for the natural sciences and for mathematics finally rescued him from the dull routine of business and sent him first to the University of Halle and then to the School of Mines at Freiburg. Here he came under the influence of the eminent geologist Abraham Gottlob Werner (1750–1817) and a lasting friendship developed between them. Mohs avidly explored every branch of practical mineralogy, even working for a time as a mine inspector in Neudorf.

Years of travel, experiment, and teaching followed, including an appointment as professor of mineralogy at Graz, during which he began to shape his own ideas for a systematic classification of minerals that would be an improvement on the "natural history method" taught by Werner. The *Versuch einer Elementarmethode zur naturhistorischen Bestimmung und Erkennen der Fossilien,* published in 1812, put forward the new method and bore the seeds of what was to be Mohs' greatest contribution, his two-volume treatise on mineralogy (*Grundriss der Mineralogie*) that appeared a decade later.

Stripped of technical terms, Mohs' scale runs as follows:

1. Talc—the softest known mineral; called soapstone for its soapy or greasy feeling
2. Gypsum—from the Greek *gúpsos,* chalk
3. Calcite—or calcium carbonate, in its transparent form called Iceland spar

4. Fluorite—calcium fluoride; glows under ultraviolet light or after heating
5. Apatite—any of a group of phosphate-bearing minerals
6. Feldspar—the moonstone is the iridescent form of this mineral
7. Quartz—silicon dioxide or silica; the name *quartz,* of unknown origin, was first applied by Agricola in 1530
8. Topaz—fluosilicate of aluminum; the handsome yellow stones turn pink when heated
9. Corundum—aluminum oxide; when red, it's a ruby, when blue, a sapphire; with iron oxides, it is the abrasive known as emery
10. Diamond—pure carbon, the hardest substance occurring naturally; from the Greek *ádámas,* invincible

By means of these ten all degrees of hardness (H) can be tested. For example, if a certain mineral can be scratched by topaz ($H = 8$) but not by quartz ($H = 7$), its hardness would lie halfway between, at 7.5.

Morgan's Raiders

A band of several thousand Confederate sympathizers under John Hunt Morgan (1825–1864), noted for their harassing tactics against Union troops during 1862 and 1863.

Tall, blue-eyed, brown-haired, mustachioed, and an excellent horseman, John Morgan was the very picture of a dashing, romantic military man. Born in Alabama and brought up in Kentucky, he had fought in the Mexican War as captain of the Kentucky Bluegrass company. On his return to Lexington he bought a hemp factory, a woolen mill, and a small number of slaves, some of whom worked in his shops—he found free Negroes "unsatisfactory." In 1857 he organized the Lexington Rifles, of which he was captain.

Morgan was greatly disappointed when Kentucky decided to remain neutral rather than secede from the Union.
Immediately after Fort Sumter he volunteered his services
to the Confederacy, wiring Jefferson Davis that he could
raise 20,000 men in Kentucky for the army. His telegram
was not answered, but he joined the Confederate army, was
made commander of a cavalry squadron, and after the
battle of Shiloh was promoted to colonel.

A few months later the raids began. Morgan's men included farmers, merchants, newspapermen, lawyers, and
doctors, as well as four of his brothers and his brother-in-
law. Their first attack in July, 1862, threatened Louisville
and Cincinnati, and opened the way for the Confederate invasion of Kentucky under General Braxton Bragg. In December the raiders struck again, this time at Hartsville,
Tennessee, a few miles south of the Kentucky state line. For
this victory Morgan was made a brigadier general. His most
spectacular move came the following year, when to cover
Bragg's advance toward Chattanooga, Morgan and a force
of some 2,500 men carried out a series of diversionary raids
through Indiana and Ohio and into Kentucky.

His luck began to run out at the battle of Portland on
July 18, 1863. Fully half his men were killed or captured,
and on the 26th Morgan surrendered to General Shackel-
ford. He was taken to the Cincinnati city jail, then transferred to the penitentiary at Columbus, from which he and
another prisoner escaped four months later by tunneling
under the wall.

In the spring of 1864 Morgan was back in Richmond,
where he was given command of a newly formed squadron
of cavalry and made responsible for all of southwestern
Virginia. By now the peak of Confederate success had been
passed. In May Sheridan had begun his drive to Atlanta,
and a month later Grant placed Richmond under siege.

Early in September, while on a reconnoitering expedition, Morgan stopped in Greeneville, Tennessee, to rest at the home of a Confederate sympathizer, Mrs. Catherine Williams, where he had been quartered before. Exactly what happened there is not clear. According to one account, as Morgan entered the house, Mrs. Williams' daughter Lucy, who was married to a Union man, left saying she was going to get some watermelons. Not long after someone shouted "The Federals are coming!" Morgan seized his gun, dashed out of the house, saw that it was surrounded and shouted, "Don't shoot. I surrender." "Hell, I know who you are," said a Union soldier, drew a bead, and fired.

Morton's Fork

(Morton's crotch or crutch). An argument in the form of a dilemma, used as a means of extracting money from the wealthy clergy during the reign of Henry VII of England.

There are two versions of the origin of the "fork." According to Erasmus, who said he got the story from Sir Thomas More in 1504, the King had called upon Bishop Richard Foxe of Winchester to enlarge the royal coffers by raising a loan from the clergy. Reluctant to part with any of their wealth, the churchmen adopted one of two ruses. Some came to the bishop dressed in the poorest of garments and pled poverty. Others donned their richest robes and argued that the cost of maintaining their offices in fitting style left nothing over. Bishop Foxe did not accept their excuses. The meanly clad, he said, must have vast stores hoarded away, which could certainly be placed at the king's disposal; the outlays of the extravagant clergy had better be curbed and their savings turned over to Henry Tudor.

Substantially the same tale was told later by Sir Francis Bacon in his *Life of Henry VII* (1622). Here the central figure is John Morton, Archbishop of Canterbury and eventually a cardinal, who in 1491 played a large part in collecting monies to help defray the expenses of Henry's war against the French. "There is a tradition," wrote Sir Francis, "of a dilemma that Bishop Morton used to raise up the Benevolences to higher rates, and some called it his 'fork' and some his 'crotch.' . . . If they [the collectors] met with any that were sparing, they should tell them that they must needs have because they laid up; and if they were spenders, they must needs have because it was seen in their port and manner of living."

Mother Carey's Chickens

The sailor's name for the stormy petrel, a web-footed sea bird related to the albatross and remarkable for its ability to fly great distances from land for days at a time; a term also applied to snow falling at sea.

The name originated with sailors from the Levant, that crescent of land forming the eastern rim of the Mediterranean and composed of Turkey, Syria, Lebanon, and Israel, but its use has been general throughout maritime circles, for petrels range over all the oceans. To ancient seamen the appearance of these sturdy gray-white birds wheeling and dipping over their ship was an especially welcome sight. It meant that the Dear Mother Mary, the *Mater Cara,* ever watchful over the men who risked their lives at sea, had sent her "chickens" as a sign that a safe harbor was not too far away.

From these seafarers too came the name *petrel,* a contraction of petrillo, little Peter. Petrels often fly so close to the crest of the waves that, with legs and feet extended, they seem to be walking on the water as the Apostle Peter is said to have done.

Napier's Bones

The first new calculating device since the abacus, consisting of a set of flat rods inscribed with digits and their multiples and arranged so as to facilitate the operations of multiplication and division. It was publicly shown before his death by the eighth Laird of Merchiston, the distinguished Scottish mathematician Sir John Napier (1550–1617), more widely known as the inventor of logarithms.

Nat Turner's Rebellion

An uprising of some 70 Negro slaves in Southampton County, Virginia, in August of 1831, led by Nat Turner (1800–1831), during which his followers killed a number of white men, women, and children. It was put down by state and Federal troops and punished by widespread reprisals, as well as the execution of 17 of the Negroes, including Turner.

It was against the law in slavery times, to teach Negroes to read and write. Nat Turner, born the property of Benjamin Turner, a small plantation owner in Southampton County, taught himself to read from the Bible, which he studied diligently. He was never an ordained preacher, but was what is known as an exhorter, and by all accounts an eloquent one. Turner found in the Holy Book the justification for his welling hatred of the condition of servitude and his fierce desire to be free.

He had run away once, in 1826 or 1827, and stayed away a month but had gone back at the promptings of a religious conscience that bade him "return to the service of [his] earthly master." In 1828 a sign came to him while he was working in the fields: "I heard a loud voice in the heavens and the spirit instantly appeared to me and said the serpent was loosened and Christ had laid down the yoke he had borne for the sins of men and that I should take it on and fight against the serpent, for the time was fast approaching when the first should be last and the last should be first."

An eclipse of the sun on February 12, 1831, convinced him that the great day was near. He confided his mission to his four most trusted friends and with them set about devising a plan which was to be carried out on July 4. Doubts and hesitations and a sudden illness of Turner's delayed them. Then on August 13 another sign put an end to uncertainty, and it was decided that the uprising would begin on Sunday the 21st.

That night a group of six Negroes, including Turner, entered the home of Joseph Travis, a former master of Turner's, killed all five members of the family and armed themselves with guns they found there. As they moved from house to house, sparing no one, other Negroes joined them. Before the night was over, the little band had swelled to about 70 men, and 55 white adults and children had lost their lives.

Turner's strategy had been to reach and hold Jerusalem (now Courtland), the county seat. But confusion in his ranks set in, and a number of state troopers and volunteers appeared to put the Negroes to flight. The state guards were followed by United States soldiers, cavalry and artillery units, and more than a hundred slaves were slain in a reign of terror that lasted until the commanding officer put a stop to it.

Eluding his pursuers at the time, Turner hid out in the woods for six weeks, sleeping by day and venturing out only at night. On October 30 his hiding place was discovered, and he gave himself up without resistance. Brought to trial, he pleaded not guilty for, as he said, he did not feel *guilty*. His *Confession,* an account of his life and the rebellion, dictated to his lawyer, Thomas R. Gray, was offered in evidence, and on November 5 Judge Jeremiah Cobb sentenced Turner to hang.

Newton's Fits

The "disposition" of rays of light, upon encountering a denser-than-air medium, such as water or glass, to be partly reflected from the surface, partly refracted (bent) as they enter the medium. This hypothesis was put forward in *Opticks* (first published in 1704) by the great English scientist Sir Isaac Newton (1642–1727).

This part of Newton's theory about the behavior of light was an attempt to resolve a dispute that began as far back as the early Greeks: Was light emitted from the sun as a stream of particles, or did it undulate toward the earth in a series of waves?

Newton noted that when sunlight fell on a pool, some of the rays were reflected from the surface while others passed through the water to reveal the bottom, an effect that seemingly could not be explained by the particle theory alone. In an attempt to find a full explanation, he postulated an ether, less dense but more elastic than air, filling all space and all matter. Then, using an analogy of the spreading ripples made by a stone dropped into water, he described a particle of light "dropped into" the ether and making "waves" that travel faster than does the particle. As the particle approaches a smooth reflecting surface, it will either be riding the crest of an ether wave or be in the trough between waves. If the former, the added impetus will create a "disposition" for the particle to enter the water and be refracted. If the latter, progress is hindered and a "disposition" for reflection will be created. It is these "dispositions" that Newton refers to as "Fits of Easy Reflexion and Easy Transmission."

Noah's Ark

The wooden vessel built at God's command in which Noah, his wife, their three sons and their wives, and a conjugal pair of every animal, bird, and creeping thing rode out the 40 days and nights of rain that flooded the earth and wiped out a mankind too wicked to be allowed to live.

Noah, whose name is derived from a root word meaning *comfort,* was 600 years old when he received the divine message. In the midst of corruption and violence that caused the Lord to regret ever having created man, Noah alone had remained upright and virtuous and was therefore worthy to be saved.

According to heavenly instructions (Genesis 6:14) the ark was to be built of gopher wood, made watertight with pitch "inside and out." Its length was to be 300 cubits (a cubit is about 18 inches), its width 50 cubits, its height 30, with the roof adding another cubit. It was to have three decks and to be divided into rooms, including a storage room for food. When all was prepared, Noah led his family and all the creatures into the ark, "and the Lord shut him in."

The torrential rains that fell are said to have been those primeval waters that God had gathered together "above the firmament" at the time of creation and now let loose. But so awful was the ensuing devastation that He at once repented of His action and, after the waters had subsided, set His rainbow in the sky as a covenant that never again would He visit such destruction upon the children of men (Genesis 9:13–17).

The tales of floods that are found in the legends of so many peoples are of course based on natural occurrences—tidal waves that overwhelm island and coastal tribes and rising rivers that inundate inland folk. The biblical account seems to be a retelling of an earlier Babylonian-Sumerian story, but modified to harmonize with the Hebrew concept of monotheism. Thus, while the heroes of the more ancient event were subsequently deified, Noah retained his human stature and lived out his days in the light of divine blessing and the injunction to "be fruitful and multiply and fill the earth."

Norman's Woe

A large sunken rock off the coast of Gloucester, Massachusetts, scene of innumerable shipwrecks; this is the "reef of Norman's Woe" in Henry Wadsworth Longfellow's ballad "The Wreck of the Hesperus."

On December 17, 1839, Longfellow wrote in his journal: "News of shipwrecks horrible on the coast. 20 bodies washed ashore near Gloucester, one lashed to a piece of the wreck. There is a reef called Norman's Woe where many of these took place; among others the schooner Hesperus. . . . I must write a ballad upon this."

Ockham's Razor

The name given to the principle of parsimony or economy in explanation, used extensively by the medieval English philosopher William of Ockham (c. 1285–1349), which holds that in accounting for any fact, nothing should be assumed that cannot be clearly established by experience or reason or that is not demanded by religious faith.

Ockham's principle is often formulated as: Entities are not to be multiplied beyond necessity (*Entia non sunt multiplicanda sine necessitate*). It seems, however, that the maxim was never stated in exactly those words. The formulations that occur most frequently in Ockham's writings are: "Plurality is not to be assumed without necessity" and

"What can be done with fewer [assumptions] is done in vain with more."

Olbers' Paradox

The contradictory fact that the sky is dark at night, although by all calculations involving star radiance it should be as bright as the surface of the sun. This was noted and examined first by the French astronomer L. P. de Chéseaux in 1744, and by the German physician and astronomer Wilhelm Olbers (1758–1840), in 1823; hence it is more correctly termed the de Chéseaux-Olbers paradox.

The paradox showed up as the result of a set of assumptions about the universe which were current in the 18th and 19th centuries. These were that the number of stars distributed throughout space is infinite and their absolute brightness is the same always and everywhere, that the stars are generally at rest, and that the universe is changeless through time.

De Chéseaux began his investigations on the basis of these assumptions. Taking the sun as a typical star of the first magnitude, he calculated the distance and size of other first-magnitude stars. Those that shone a quarter as bright, he reasoned, would be twice the distance away and their apparent diameter halved; but there would be four times as many of them (on the hypothesis of even distribution), and the amount of sky they occupied would be the same as that of the first-magnitude stars. Thus the sky at all times should be filled with a total radiance as great as the sun's. That this was obviously not so he explained by assuming the existence of an interstellar fluid in which much of the light was lost.

Following de Chéseaux by three-quarters of a century, Olbers assumed the presence, between the earth and the stars, of large amounts of very fine dust that absorbed the extra light.

Since then, and especially from 1920 on, it has been regarded as established that the universe is expanding. Accordingly, the light received from galaxies moving at high velocities farther out into space is very much weakened, and the amount of light falling upon any one point in space is so reduced that the night sky is dark.

Mrs. O'Leary's Cow

The ill-starred animal who, on the night of October 8, 1871, is said to have kicked over a lantern in Mrs. O'Leary's barn behind the dwelling at 137 De Koven Street on Chicago's West Side, thus starting a disastrous fire that wiped out the entire business district and took an enormous toll in lives and property.

> One dark night—when people were in bed,
>   Old Mrs. Leary lit a lantern in her shed.
> The cow kicked it over, winked its eye, and said,
> There'll be a hot time in the old town tonight.
>
>   —ANON.

The Chicago fire has been called the most destructive of its kind in American history: 3½ acres of houses and business buildings in the heart of the city totally destroyed; 300 persons dead; 90,000 left homeless; 200 million dollars of property damage.

In the summer of 1871 Chicago stood dangerously vulnerable to any random spark. Her streets were paved with pine blocks, her sidewalks were of well-seasoned wood; pine and hemlock fences separated adjoining properties, and in many instances blocked access to the river. There were 17 grain elevators dotted among the paint and varnish shops, lumber mills, and woodworking plants in the industrial area. Almost every dwelling had its little leanto,

shed, or barn where kindling was stored and where the
family cow, goat, sheep, or flock of chickens was housed.
There had been no rain for three months.

The first week of October might have been a dress re-
hearsal for the main event. There had been a number of
small fires, none of them serious, in various parts of town;
and then on Saturday, October 7, a woodworking factory
blazed up and burned until early Sunday morning. In the
course of fighting it several pieces of apparatus were put
out of commission and the firemen were exhausted.

Just how the O'Leary fire started has never been as-
certained. The crucial fact seems to be that the fire did
start in the O'Leary barn, and that whoever was responsible, if anyone was, did not raise an immediate alarm, so
that within minutes the blaze was out of control.

One curious circumstance remains. When the flames were
finally quenched and the smoke had lifted, there in the
midst of a black-charred wasteland stood a little clump of
houses including the O'Leary's, whole and quite un-
harmed.

Orion's Belt

(Orion's girdle; Jacob's staff, *which see*). Three stars
in a straight line within the great quadrangle of the constellation Orion.

In Greek mythology Orion, son of Poseidon and Eury-
ales, was a mighty hunter. According to one story, he once
met Artemis, sister of Apollo and herself a devotee of the
chase, and they went hunting together. Apollo, concerned
for his sister's virginity, sent a huge scorpion after Orion
who dived into the sea. When only the swimmer's head was
visible far off above the waves, Apollo by a trick caused
Artemis to loose an arrow which killed Orion. Overcome
with grief and unable to bring Orion back to life, Artemis

placed his image in the heavens. There, as the constellation Orion, with his favorite hunting dog (Canis Major; *see* Orion's hound), he is forever stalked by the Scorpion.

Orion's Hound

The hunting dog that accompanied Orion on his expeditions (*see* Orion's belt). When Orion was slain and his image placed in the sky as a constellation, the animal was similarly commemorated and became Canis Major, faithfully following at his master's heel.

Canis Major is distinguished for displaying (at the nose of the imaginary figure) the most brilliant star in the heavens, Sirius, the Dog Star. *Sirius* comes from the Greek word for *scorching*. At the time of year when the star rises with the sun, which occurs about the middle of July, the ancients would brace themselves for a season of sultry, sticky heat.

Later, the Romans named this hottest part of the year *Dies caniculares,* literally, dog days. Besides physical discomfort, they also brought fevers and pestilence, disasters which the city fathers sought to avert by sacrificing a dog, often specifically a red one, to the baleful Sirius.

Pandora's Box

A casket containing all the evils of the earth and belonging to Pandora, the first woman, according to mythology, to come into the world of men.

The Greek myth tells that Prometheus (Forethought) stole fire from the gods and gave it to man. Zeus despised mankind and had deliberately withheld the precious gift. In anger he counteracted the great benefit thus bestowed by ordering Hephaestus, god of the forge, to create a woman, who was thereupon endowed by the gods and goddesses with gifts of beauty and many skills (Pandora, All-gifts). She was sent to Epimetheus (Afterthought), brother of Prometheus, to be his bride; and with her went a box in which Prometheus had confined the host of troubles that might plague the world.

Epimetheus had been warned by his brother never to accept anything from Zeus but ignored the warning and married Pandora. He did follow Prometheus' advice by forbidding Pandora to open the box. One day when Epimetheus was away, Pandora's curiosity got the better of her, and she pried open the lid. Immediately the imprisoned host of evils streamed out into the world, where they have been playing havoc ever since. Last out of the box was a gauzy-winged creature named Hope. Some say that with his customary foresight Prometheus had slipped her too into the box, so that if the worst happened, all might not be lost.

Parkinson's Disease

(*Paralysis agitans*, shaking palsy). A disease generally of older people, marked by a masklike facial expression (Parkinsonian mask), tremors of the limbs, and a shuffling gait, progressing to a state of physical helplessness. It was described in 1817 by the English surgeon and paleontologist James Parkinson (1755–1844).

There is one not very well-known facet to Parkinson's career. In 1794 he was haled before the Privy Council and examined under oath for his suspected part in the "Popgun plot," an attempt against the life of George III. According to the charges, the king was to have been assassinated by a poisoned blow dart while attending a performance at a London theater. The examination revealed nothing more than that Parkinson was a member and corresponding secretary of the London Corresponding Society, one of many reform groups of that decade inspired by the French Revolution and dedicated to Parliamentary reform, and he was exonerated.

Pascal's Amulet

Two copies of a brief devotional passage (one on parchment enclosing a second on paper) written by the French mathematician Blaise Pascal (1623–1662) and always carried on his person after he had undergone an intense religious experience on the night of November 23, 1654.

Pascal's religious experience, his "night of fire," came after a particularly harrowing physical experience. He was driving in a coach to Neuilly, a suburb of Paris, and was nearing one of the many bridges over the Seine. Suddenly the horses bolted and leaped over the parapet. If the traces had not snapped Pascal would have been dragged to his death.

That night the revelation occurred, "from about half-past ten in the evening until about half-past twelve," according to the lines contained in the amulet. The overwhelming emotion never left Pascal, and he devoted the rest of his life almost entirely to religious activities.

So brilliant were the philosophical and religious works of these last years—the *Pensées,* the defense of the Jansenist Arnauld in the *Lettres provinciales,* and others—that they tend to overshadow the remarkable mathematical and scientific accomplishments that preceded his conversion. As a boy Pascal was a prodigy. At the age of 12, without instruction, he began working out the principles of geometry on his own. At 16 he had produced his first major work, *Essai pour les coniques,* published in 1640. Two years later, as an aid to his father's tax work, he invented a calculating machine (*see* Babbage's analytical engine).

Other significant contributions followed, including the

famous series of experiments on air pressure that disproved
the ancient doctrine that "Nature abhors a vacuum."

Paul Revere's Ride

The celebrated cross-country gallop (made famous by
Longfellow's poem of the same name) from Charlestown
to Lexington on the night of April 18, 1775, by the express
courier, Paul Revere (1735–1818), to warn the colonists
of approaching British troops.

An official courier for the Boston Committee of Correspondence in the troubled years before the Revolutionary
War, Paul Revere had been carrying messages up and
down the Eastern seaboard.

There had been rumors for some days that British troops
under General Gage in Boston were about to make some
sort of move. Gage had heard there was a store of gun-
powder in Concord and planned to take possession of it.
The question for the Continentals was whether the redcoats
would march overland from Boston or attempt a surprise
landing farther up the Massachusetts coast. Once this was
determined, the lantern signal—"One if by land and two if
by sea"—was to be flashed from the Old North Church tower,
and the alarm would go out.

By all accounts, including his own, Revere already knew
that the British would move by sea. The signals, placed in
the belfry by a member of the Sons of Liberty named Robert
Newman, were for the benefit of other patriots waiting on
the Charlestown shore. Revere himself had been sent for
earlier that evening by Dr. Joseph Warren, president of the
Massachusetts provincial congress, and instructed to ride
to Lexington and warn John Adams and John Hancock of
the danger. At the same time Dr. Warren had dispatched
another rider, William Dawes, direct to Lexington.

Revere stopped long enough to make sure the signals

had been seen, then borrowed the horse Brown Beauty from Dean John Larkin and raced off for the Reverend Clark's house where Adams and Hancock were staying.

"About midnight," wrote William Monroe, an orderly sergeant on guard at Clark's, "Colonel Paul Revere rode up and requested admittance. I told him the family had just retired and requested that they might not be disturbed by any noise about the house.

" 'Noise!' said he. 'You'll have noise enough before long. The regulars are coming out.'

"We then permitted him to pass."

Although Longfellow's poem has Revere finishing his ride in Concord, Revere was picked up by British scouts while still on the road, held for some hours for questioning and grudgingly released.

Peck's Bad Boy

The incorrigible Hennery, whose pranks attained nationwide popularity, was created in 1882 by George Wilbur Peck (1840–1916), newspaper editor and twice governor of Wisconsin.

For a number of years and with indifferent success Peck had been running a weekly newspaper, first in La Crosse and then in Milwaukee. *Peck's Sun* was "more a collection of editorial humor than a newspaper in the modern sense"; and the sketches about Hennery the Bad Boy and the tricks he played on his ever-tipsy pa might at first have just seemed more of the same. He lined pa's hatband with limburger cheese; soaked pa's handkerchief in rum and stuffed it full of playing cards the day the old man had been coaxed into going to church; tattled on him to ma until she lit out after the poor fellow with a broomstick. In an age when the practical joke was a high form of amusement, the characters caught on and circulation shot up. In 1883 a

Chicago publisher brought out a first and then a second series of the stories, and Americans laughed over them for the next 40 years.

Penn's Woods

The state of Pennsylvania, founded in 1681 by the Quaker William Penn (1644–1718), son of Admiral William Penn, as a refuge from religious and legal persecution.

Penn established his colony in America on the principle that sound government demands complete liberty of conscience. The tract of land that was to provide a haven for his ideas had been deeded by Charles II in repayment of a 16,000-pound loan to the King by Penn's father. It comprised 48,000 square miles, rich in minerals and very fertile, bounded on the east by the Delaware River and running from the Maryland line "northward as far as plantable," which carried the northwest border all the way up to Lake Erie.

The petition was filed in 1680 and granted in 1681. Penn proposed to name the territory Sylvania. Charles insisted on prefixing Penn in honor of the admiral. Over the son's strenuous objection, including an attempt to bribe the secretaries into altering the inscription, the King's will prevailed.

Peter's Pence

A tribute to the Pope of a penny a year from each English household, paid from the 7th or 8th century A.D. until abolished by Henry VIII in 1534.

The origin of this ecclesiastical tax, called Peter's pence, Peter's penny or Peterpenny, is not too clear. Imposition of the tax has been variously attributed to Ine (688–728), king of Wessex in southern England, and to Offa (755–796), ruler of the one-time kingdom of Mercia in central

England. It is known that the latter was on friendly terms with Pope Adrian I, by whose good offices a program of clerical reforms advantageous to Offa was carried through. Perhaps the penny tax was instituted in gratitude. (The English word penny replaced the older Latin *denarius,* which survived as the sign *d,* and was originally written *pending.*)

There is no known written reference to the tax prior to 1031, and by then it is mentioned as required by a law already ancient. According to statute, the tax was to be paid by every family having land worth 30 pence rental a year and was due on August 1, the feast of St. Peter; hence the name. Another designation for the levy was hearth tax, and there is a little 13th century verse which runs:

> From rome he broghte an heste that me here nome
> Petres peni of ech hous that smoke out of come.

On several occasions the English, in order to wrest concessions from the Pope, withheld the tax or threatened to do so. When the crisis subsided, the tax was restored. In the reign of Henry VIII, however, open warfare broke out between church and state. Pope Clement VII refused to sanction Henry's divorce from Catherine of Aragon, so that he might marry Anne Boleyn, whereupon the monarch and Parliament declared complete separation from Rome and a transfer of all church funds to the crown. Thus ended the English tribute.

After 1860, the term Peter's pence came to be used only for voluntary contributions made by Roman Catholics to the papal treasury.

Pick's Pike

The Ledo Road, built under the supervision of the American Brigadier General Lewis A. Pick, to serve as an alternate to the interdicted Burma Road. It became famous during World War II as the supply route from Lashio, Burma, into southwest China.

Keeping open a military supply line into China, in the face of Japanese control of Burma, was one of the most taxing problems of the Eastern theater of operations. The 700-mile Burma Road, from Kunming to Lashio in the central plains, had been built (1937–1939) during the Sino-Japanese war after all of China's supply ports had been closed off. Together with a rail line south from Lashio to the port of Rangoon, the Burma Road provided necessary access. When the Japanese overran Burma and captured Lashio in March, 1942, the road had to be abandoned, and outside aid was generally confined to what could be moved by the important but inadequate air lift "over the hump" from India to China.

In December, 1942, however, United States Army engineers began construction of an alternate road down from the north, starting at Ledo in eastern Assam province, India, and curving south and east to join the Burma Road just after it crossed the border into China. The way lay through enemy territory, but under orders from General "Vinegar Joe" Stilwell, then in command as assistant to Generalissimo Chiang Kai-shek, a Chinese troop division was deployed to clear the way ahead of the bulldozers and pick-and-shovel gangs. Because of jungle, heat, malaria, and a monsoon season that dumped 150 inches of rain during its half-year span, the road in ten months had crawled only as far as the Naga Hills, some 45 miles out of Ledo. On October 13, 1943, leadership of the project was transferred to Brigadier General Lewis A. Pick, and the work began to move again. White-haired and with bright blue eyes, Pick, a native of Auburn, Alabama, came from the Engineer Corps of the United States Army, had worked with the Missouri River Division of the corps at Omaha,

Nebraska, and had drawn up the plan for flood control of the Missouri waterway. Once in command, he soon put into operation his formula for exacting top performance: meticulous planning, plenty of good food, stoves in the living quarters, movies whenever possible, and his own rugged confidence that the job could be done. The Burma Road junction was 420 miles away. Following a route laid out by aerial reconnaissance, Pick and his men reached it in just 15 months.

Pick's close personal involvement with all phases of the work left an indelible imprint. It was not long before both laborers and soldiers began talking about Pick's Pike, and the name stuck even after Ledo Road was officially changed, at Chiang's suggestion, to Stilwell Road.

Pike's Peak

One of the highest (14,140 feet) of the mountain peaks in the Rampart range of the Rocky Mountains in central Colorado, discovered by Captain Zebulon Montgomery Pike (1779–1813) in November, 1806.

"At 2 o'clock in the afternoon," wrote Captain Pike in his diary under the date of November 15, 1806, "I thought I could distinguish a mountain to our right, which appeared like a small blue cloud; viewed it with a spy glass and was still more confirmed in my conjecture . . . in half an hour they appeared in full view before us." The "they" were a range Pike refers to as the Mexican Mountains, while the one likened to a cloud was the towering summit later to bear his name.

At the time this was written the Captain was heading a little military band commissioned by President Jefferson to explore the country west and southwest of St. Louis and to treat with the Indian tribes in the area. Having moved westward along the Arkansas River as far as Pueblo, Pike and his men left the waterway and struck off in a northerly direction on an overland side trip.

It took more than a week to reach the foothills and begin the climb. After making a few observations—the rocks showed no signs of animal or vegetable life and the temperature was 4° below zero—the party returned to Pueblo to continue their expedition. This ended some weeks later at a stockade established by Pike at Rio Conejos, where he and his men were captured by the Spaniards and sent first to Santa Fe and then to Chihuahua, being finally released at the American frontier in July, 1807. According to Elliott Coues, who edited Pike's diary, there is some evidence that the Captain deliberately invited seizure by the Spanish authorities in order to spy on their garrisons.

The following year Pike was promoted to major, and by 1812 had attained the rank of full colonel. When the war with England broke out he went into active service as adjutant and inspector general. At the battle of York (Toronto), while leading an assault on a British stronghold, he was fatally injured by a piece of rock from a magazine exploded by the retreating enemy.

Pike never did climb to the top of his mountain, nor did it bear his name during his lifetime. The summit was first reached in July, 1820, by a group of four men headed by Dr. Edwin James, and for some years thereafter it was known as James' Peak. In the 1830s, however, people began to speak of it as Pike's Peak, and by midcentury the name had been made official.

Plato's Cave

An allegory used by the Greek philosopher Plato (428/427–348/347 B.C.) in Chapter VII of *The Republic* to elucidate the nature of reality and to show how enlightened philosopher-kings may come to know it and thus be equipped to rule by right of their superior knowledge.

In *The Republic,* which takes the form of a dialogue between Socrates and two young men, Plato sets out to describe the ideal state. In order to clarify the nature of reality and our knowledge of it, he has Socrates compare our situation to that of men living in a huge cave, who are chained so as to be able to look only toward the back of the cave. Behind them and invisible to them passes a procession of other men carrying all sorts of objects, the shadows of which are cast on the back wall of the cave. Knowing nothing else, the chained men take the shadows to be all that is real and worthwhile and live their lives accordingly.

If, however, one of the men should break his fetters and come out of the cave into the sunlight, he would see the real world and all its objects in their true forms and colors, and would understand the falseness and unreality he had escaped from. It would then be his duty to go back into the cave and teach his fellow men the truth.

It is such men—and women too—able to ascend into the sunlight of reason and true understanding who become the philosophers, standing far above those "who fight one another for shadows." Rigorously educated and constantly screened through years of training, only those who survive the tests are finally to be considered worthy to hold public office and to rule in the ideal state.

Playfair's Axiom

A reformulation of Euclid's famous Fifth Postulate, proposed by the Scottish physicist and mathematician John Playfair (1748–1819), author of *Elements of Geometry* and an ordained minister.

Euclid's system of geometry, as set forth in his *Elements* (*c.* 300 B.C.), rests on a number of axioms and postulates.

One of these, originally listed as Axiom 12, has come to be known as the fifth or parallel postulate. It states that if a straight line crosses two other straight lines so that the sum of the two interior angles on the same side is less than two right angles, then the two lines, when extended indefinitely, will meet on the side where the two interior angles are less than two right angles.

Two thousand years and many reformulations later, John Playfair gave the postulate essentially the form in which every high-school student encounters it today: two intersecting straight lines cannot both be parallel to a third straight line; or, through a given point in a given plane, only one straight line can be drawn parallel to a given straight line.

Poisson's Ratio

The relation of sidewise strain to lengthwise strain in material subjected to extension or compression, expressed as a fraction that is constant for each type of material and varying from $\frac{1}{5}$ to $\frac{1}{2}$ for different kinds of material. The ratio was calculated by the celebrated French mathematician Siméon Denis Poisson (1781–1840).

Poor Richard's Almanack

A popular annual, published by Benjamin Franklin (1706–1790) under the pseudonym Richard Saunders, which dispensed homely wisdom and practical advice to its subscribers from 1732 to 1757.

Franklin's purpose in putting out his almanac was simple. Observing that his neighbors generally read few books, he filled "all the little spaces that occurr'd between the remarkable days in the calendar with proverbial sentences, chiefly such as inculcated industry and frugality, as the means of procuring wealth, and thereby securing virtue."

Both "entertaining and useful," the *Almanack* was looked forward to eagerly by its 10,000 or so subscribers. While the sayings for which Richard was famous often originated with other authors, in passing through Franklin's hands they received an imprint that made them seem native and familiar. "Heaven ne'er helps the man who will not act," a fragment from Sophocles, became "God helps those who help themselves," a sentiment any frontiersman could appreciate. "Forewarned, forearmed" and "Diligence is the mother of good luck," were taken from Cervantes' *Don Quixote*.

"Search others for their virtues, thyself for thy vices" and "a good conscience is a continual Christmas," whatever their origins, convey the spirit of Quaker fellowship; "God heals, the doctor takes the fee," a bit of the Franklin humor.

Potiphar's Wife

The amorous spouse of an officer in Pharaoh's army who tried to seduce Joseph, then serving as a slave in her husband's household.

The Book of Genesis tells how Joseph, the favorite son of Jacob, had incurred the jealousy of his brothers and had been sold to a passing caravan of Midianites. These, in turn, traveled to Egypt and sold Joseph to Potiphar, a captain of Pharaoh's guard. Recognizing Joseph's abilities, Potiphar made him overseer of his household; and Potiphar's wife, Zuleika, struck by Joseph's bearing and charm, set out to win his affections.

Mindful of his duties to his master and to God, Joseph courteously but firmly rejected her advances. Zuleika, inflamed by passion, continued to pursue him. One day, when no one else was about, she caught hold of his garment and sought to draw him into the bedroom; whereupon Joseph "left his garment in her hand, and fled and got out of the house."

Now furious, Zuleika took the garment to her husband as proof that Joseph had tried to take advantage of her. Potiphar ordered Joseph thrown into prison, and there he stayed until, having interpreted Pharaoh's dream about the seven fat cows and the seven lean cows and the fat and thin ears of wheat, he was released and given authority to prepare Egypt to meet the famine foretold by the dreams.

There is an apocryphal retelling of the Joseph-Zuleika episode. In it there is a torn fragment, rather than the whole garment, that Zuleika shows her husband. Here also Zuleika is named, for she is nameless in the bible story. The account goes on to say that when Potiphar's wife showed her husband the bit of cloth, the babe in the cradle spoke up and said: "Look carefully, O Potiphar. If it was torn from the front of Joseph's garment, he was pursuing her, but if from the back, she was pursuing him." Potiphar looked and saw that it was indeed from the back and that Joseph was blameless. Some time later Zuleika contrived, it is not said how, to have Joseph imprisoned.

Put's Hill

(Putnam's Hill). A dangerously steep incline in the town of Greenwich, Connecticut, down which General Israel Putnam rode on horseback at breakneck speed to avoid being cornered and captured by the British during the Revolutionary War.

In the winter of 1778–1779, when the northern wing of the Continental Army was being harried by British soldiers fanning out from New York, Major General Israel Putnam was in command of troops quartered in the area between Reading, Connecticut, and the New York state line. On February 26 the General was in the little town of Greenwich, then called Horseneck, where according to one account he was staying with General Ebeneezer Mead, a member of the Committee of Safety. At about nine o'clock in the morning a band of Tory raiders under General Tryon entered the town. The story has it that Putnam glimpsed their red coats in his shaving mirror, and "half shaven and with lather still on his face," dashed out to rally forces and give battle.

The handful of Continentals fought bravely, but Putnam soon saw that they were no match for the superior British numbers, and reinforcements were needed. Bidding his men scatter and find safety in a nearby swamp, he jumped on his horse and raced down the main street, headed for Stamford 5 miles away. Diverted from their original quarry, the British took off after the General. They were gaining rapidly when Putnam suddenly swerved his horse from the road and galloped up a hill on whose summit stood a small Episcopal church overlooking an almost sheer drop to the little valley below. Years before, a series of stones had been set into the steep hillside from top to bottom, forming a rough staircase, and down these steps, all seventy or more of them, clattered Putnam.

Stunned at thus seeing their prize escape, but not daring to follow, the redcoats sent one or two half-hearted volleys after the fleeing horseman. One bullet pierced his army hat, but no further damage is recorded. Putnam reached Stamford safely, the reserves were dispatched in time, and the British contingent was thoroughly routed.

Queen Anne's Bounty

The name for a fund created by the English Queen Anne (1665–1714), intended to supplement the livings of the poorer clergy.

For several hundred years it had been customary for the

Roman Catholic clergy to turn over to Rome all the profits from the first year of a new parish appointment or preferment and yearly thereafter a tenth of such profits, the former called first fruits or *annates,* the latter *decimae.* When Henry VIII broke with the Pope in 1534 these payments, along with Peter's pence (*which see*), were diverted to the crown coffers.

In 1704 Queen Anne, who was intensely anti-Catholic but at the same time extremely religious, granted a charter for the bounty, which in effect utilized contributions from the richer parishes to eke out the revenues of those bringing in 50 pounds a year or less. By a Parliamentary measure passed in 1926, the fund was gradually retired.

Queen Anne's Free Gift

An annual grant of money, instituted by Queen Anne (1665–1714), earmarked for ships' surgeons and used to supplement the twopence monthly fee they collected for each man aboard.

Queen Anne's Lace

(Wild carrot [*Daucus carota*]). A tough, weedy plant of the herb family Umbelliferae (umbrella- or shade-bearing). Its blossom, a flat, circular cluster of tiny white florets with an occasional dot of purple is set in a delicate lacelike pattern reminiscent of the court ruffs and flounces fashionable in Queen Anne's day.

The relatives of this royal weed are legion. Numbering some 2,500 species, they are found in all temperate zones of the world and include both edible and poisonous varieties. Among the edible are carrots, parsley, celery, and parsnips, and such savory herbs as dill, anise, and caraway. The roots and fruit of water hemlock, fool's parsley, and the like contain deadly alkaloids; it may have been an infusion of one of these that filled the "cup of hemlock" used to carry out the death sentence against the philosopher Socrates.

Queen Mary's Thistle

The purple-headed *Onopordon acanthium* or cotton thistle, so-called because it is covered with small, thread-like white hairs. It is the national flower of Scotland.

In florigraphy, the language of flowers (first developed by the Greeks), the thistle stands for austerity, a trait some consider characteristic of the land it symbolizes. Apparently the royal prefix was added near the end of the 16th century, referring to the occasion when a group of attendants were supposed to have presented a handful of the wild-flowers to Mary, Queen of Scots (1542–1587), then imprisoned in Fotheringay castle by her cousin Elizabeth.

Rama's Bridge

(Adam's bridge). A series of small, sandy islets spanning the gap between the island of Rameswaram, off the southeastern coast of India, and the island of Mannar, near the northeastern coast of Ceylon.

In the *Rāmāyana,* one of the two great Hindu epics (the other is the *Mahābharata*), the story is told that the string of islets was once part of a huge causeway built for the hero Rāmā, son of King Daśaratha. Rāmā's wife, Sītā, had been kidnaped from India by the Demon King Rāvana and carried across the Strait of Mannar to his capital Lankā in Ceylon. Rāmā and his brother set out to rescue her, and after many adventures reached the Indian coast. An alliance was made with Sugrīva, King of the Monkeys, who sent an army commanded by the monkey-general Hanumān, to help Rāmā. Gathering great boulders and uprooting trees, the monkeys built a bridge across the straits. Rāmā and his allies crossed over, slew the Demon King, and brought Sītā safely home.

A more mundane account has the Indian and Ceylonese land masses originally connected by a sandy neck of land some 30 miles long. Then in 1480, according to temple records, the area was battered by a furious tropical storm that washed away most of the isthmus and left nothing but the scattering of sandbanks known today.

Raynaud's Disease

A disorder characterized by constriction of the smallest blood vessels of the extremities, so that the fingers and toes, and sometimes the nose and ears as well, become blue (cyanosed) and very cold. It is essentially an idiopathic condition (that is, self-originated or without known cause), but one that can be brought on by extremes of cold or emotional tension, females being more susceptible. The syndrome was first described by the French surgeon Maurice Raynaud (1834–1881).

Ringer's Solution

A solution of sodium, potassium, and calcium, among other ingredients, in the approximate proportions found in frog's blood, in which the English physician, Sidney Ringer, was able in 1882 to keep a frog's heart alive and beating outside its body.

Robert's Rules of Order

A manual of parliamentary procedure, first published in 1876, written by Brigadier General Henry Martyn Robert (1837–1923) of Robertville, South Carolina.

"Where there is no law, but each man does what is right in his own eyes, there is the least of liberty," wrote General Robert. His famous *Rules* were intended to provide a maximum of liberty within a necessary framework of order. The son of a minister, Robert had graduated from the United States Military Academy at 20 (he was an acting assistant professor during his senior year), and, after serving all through the Civil War on the Union side, returned to the Academy (1865–1867) to take charge of the department of military engineering. His experience and talents in that field were later put to use when he took part in designing a sea wall 17 feet high and 7½ miles long to protect Galveston from Gulf floods, and a 2-mile causeway (finished in 1909) to connect that island city with the Texas mainland.

The first edition of the *Rules of Order* was a modest one, 4,000 copies "enough to last two years," Robert estimated. That should be ample time, he felt, to test the efficiency of the manual and to produce criticism useful for a revised edition. In 1893 a revised edition appeared, and another in 1915; the 75th-anniversary printing that came out in 1951 is based on the 1915 plates.

As a guide to the best use of his manual, Robert appended a study outline. Suggesting that classes be formed among an organization's members, he recommended that the simplest rules be learned first, and added that it is better to know how to find a correct ruling than to worry about memorizing it.

Robin Hood's Barn

"All around Robin Hood's barn" is said of any roundabout way of getting to a point or place and probably stems from the merry chase Robin Hood led the Sheriff of Nottingham in the latter's effort to capture the greenwood bandit who loved to "take from the rich to give to the poor."

Roget's Thesaurus

A collection of English words and phrases arranged according to the ideas they express, rather than in alphabetical order, published in 1852 by the English physician and lecturer Peter Mark Roget (1779–1869), and offered "to facilitate the expression of ideas and to assist in literary composition."

As Roget noted in the introduction to the first edition of the *Thesaurus,* his was not the first attempt at such a compilation. The earliest, dating from about the 10th century, is the *Amera Cósha,* or *Vocabulary of the Sanskrit Language* (a translation was published in 1808), somewhat confused but "exhibiting a remarkable effort at analysis at so remote a period of Indian literature." A more orderly classification, in Roget's opinion, was to be found in the 17th-century work of Bishop John Wilkins, *An Essay towards a Real Character and a Philosophical Language* (*see* Wilkins' Real Character); but the schema of symbols that accompanied it was too complicated and artificial to be useful. The same criticism applied to an anonymous French work that appeared in 1797.

In his own system Roget took the classifications of natural history as his guiding principle. Words were divided into categories in the same way that plants and animals had been divided into families. As genus branched off into related but differing species, so the meanings of words shaded into other meanings related but not the same. A particular innovation was the inclusion of phrases synonymous with single words for which no individual or one-word synonyms existed.

This ambitious work, which might have been a life-time project for another man, was merely the capstone of Roget's long and versatile career. He was born in London of a Swiss father and an English mother. A graduate of Edinburgh

Medical School at 19, he spent the next 40 years tutoring, practicing medicine, and lecturing, first on animal physiology, then on the theory and practice of medicine. He was one of the founders of the Manchester Medical School and the first to hold the Fullerian professorship of physiology at the Royal Institution. He wrote treatises on electricity, galvanism, and electromagnetism; he tried to make a calculating machine; he devised a successful slide rule for performing mathematical operations of involution (raising a number to any power) and evolution (extracting any root of a number); and besides designing a pocket chessboard, found the first complete solution to the knight's move—to start on a given square, to visit every square once only, and to end on a given square of a different color.

Roosevelt's Rough Riders

The First Volunteer Cavalry, organized by Theodore Roosevelt (1858–1919) and Leonard Wood (1860–1927) just after the outbreak of the Spanish-American War in April, 1898.

The battleship *Maine* was blown up in Havana harbor on February 15, 1898, and was the occasion for a war that sections of the press had been bent upon for several years. Among those most eager to "punish Spain" was the former president of the New York Police Board and recently appointed Assistant Secretary of the Navy, Theodore Roosevelt. He resigned his government post and immediately tendered his services.

After war was actually declared on April 25, Congress authorized the formation of three cavalry regiments, and Roosevelt was offered command of one of them. He elected instead to serve as lieutenant colonel under Colonel Wood, an army surgeon and former captain. Together the men issued a call for volunteers which was answered with a rush of applications, and by May 1 a training camp had been set up at San Antonio, Texas.

The Rough Riders, a name bestowed by newspaper correspondents and somewhat of an embarrassment to the commanders, were an unlikely assemblage. From the West came the cowboys of Roosevelt's ranching days and even a few reformed "bad men"; from the East, steeplechase riders, polo players, and members of swank New York college clubs. An air of informality permeated the outfit. Colonel Wood was the proper military man of discipline and drill, but Roosevelt's boyish enthusiasms and huge delight in the enterprise kept breaking through.

Just getting to Cuba at all was a problem, and it was solved with typical Roosevelt élan. When the Rough Riders reached their embarkation point at Tampa on June 8, they found that the transport assigned to them, the U.S.S. *Yucatan*, was scheduled to carry two other regiments that would fill her to capacity, but that these had not yet arrived. Roosevelt got his men out of their train and onto the gangplank in double-quick time; and while "there was a good deal of expostulation," he wrote later, "we had possession."

Trouble and disorganization continued to dog the troops. The landing on the Cuban coast was made in high surf and two of the men drowned. Once ashore, orders sent out by one leader were ignored by another. A signal-corps balloon, hoisted to look for an auxiliary trail through the heavy underbrush, gave away the American position, which was subjected to withering fire.

The charge up San Juan Hill on July 1, high point of the campaign, was actually the storming of Kettle Hill, some little distance from the San Juan fortifications. Roosevelt, on horseback and wearing a sombrero draped with a blue polka-dotted handkerchief, was everywhere, shouting encouragement and recklessly disregarding the enemy. He was luckier than many who followed him. Casualties among the Rough Riders, he estimated later, were seven times those of the other volunteer units. But Kettle Hill was taken, and San Juan Hill soon after; the port of Santiago was cut off by land and blockaded by sea. On July 3 the entire Spanish fleet was destroyed as it tried to slip out of the harbor, and the war was essentially over. Shortly afterward, Santiago surrendered formally, and on August 12 Spain signed a preliminary peace treaty.

Three days later the returning American regiments landed at Montauk, Long Island, for mustering out; and in September Roosevelt reluctantly bade farewell to his men.

Russell's Paradox

That a class (or set) whose members are all and only those classes that are not members of themselves can be proven both to be and not to be a member of itself. This contradiction was discovered in 1901 by the distinguished English philosopher Bertrand Russell (b. 1872) in the course of his studies in logic and the foundations of mathematics.

Consider, for example, the class of all entities. In a sense, this class itself is an entity; therefore it is a member of itself. On the other hand, take any ordinary class, that of animals, for instance. Obviously the class of all animals is not itself an animal and hence is not a member of itself.

Now consider a class (call it R) whose *members* are the *classes* that are not members of themselves. What about the class R itself? Is R a member of R? Clearly, if it is a member of itself, then it cannot be a member of itself, since R consists only of classes that are not members of themselves. But if it is not a member of itself, then it must be a

member of itself, since *R* consists of all those classes that
are not members of themselves.

This is what Russell called The Contradiction.

Saint Agnes' Eve

January 20, the night on which, by practicing certain
rituals, a young girl would dream of the man whom she was
to marry.

The "Eve of St. Agnes" by John Keats, alludes to some
of the ancient strictures laid on hopeful maidens, such as
going supperless to bed and being careful not to look sidewise or over the shoulder but only straight ahead.

Saint Agnes herself, vowed to chastity from childhood,
had suffered martyrdom at 13 in 304 A.D. during the reign
of Diocletian, for having refused to marry the son of the
prefect Sempronius.

Saint Andrew's Cross

An X-shaped cross on which the Apostle Andrew, the
brother of Peter, was crucified. The name also refers to a
four-petaled wildflower related to St.-John's-wort (*which
see*).

Saint Anthony's Cross

The tau, or T-shaped cross, also called Egyptian
crutch, the symbol of Egyptian-born St. Anthony, the Abbot (*see* Saint Anthony's Fire).

Saint Anthony's Fire

Common name for erysipelas, a very painful bacterial
infection, especially of the face, during which the skin becomes fiery red and swollen. It is also called *burning sick-
ness, hellfire,* and *sacred fire.*

The cult of St. Anthony (*c*. 251–*c*. 356 A.D.), Egyptian-born abbot who lived an extraordinarily ascetic life, first took form in the 11th century. At the time large areas of Europe were being swept by an epidemic, often fatal, marked by inflamed, itching skin and occasionally gangrene. During this period of affliction St. Anthony's relics were moved from Egypt to a final resting place in France, and the belief sprang up that it was he who was interceding for the sufferers.

Although Saint Anthony's fire was later identified with erysipelas, the severe effects of the disease were more closely allied with those of ergotism, a disorder that often leads to gangrene and is caused by the use of flour from grains, rye in particular, which have been blighted by the fungus ergot.

Saint Catherine's Wheel

A large wheel studded with razor-sharp knives, to which the Roman Emperor Marcus Aurelius Maxentius ordered Catherine of Alexandria (*c*. 310) bound for execution.

According to saintly legend, Catherine was a handsome woman, young, of unusual learning, and a devout Christian. Having angered the emperor Maxentius by reproving him for his pagan ways, she was commanded to appear before him and defend her faith against 50 savants of the realm. Her argument was so skillful that all 50 confessed themselves defeated, whereupon the emperor ordered them to the stake. He then tried to seduce Catherine, offering to put aside his legal wife, Faustina. When Catherine rejected him, he had her cast into prison and flogged with oxhide lashes. Faustina with a retinue of 200 went to the prison where Catherine converted them all. Maxentius heard of the visit and put the entire party to death. The fatal wheel was then prepared, but when Catherine was bound to it, the wheel broke and the knives flew among the spectators, maiming and killing many of them. The executioner then struck off the saint's head with a sword, at which angels descended and carried the body off to Mount Sinai.

An account that comes to us from the ecclesiastical historian Eusebius of Caesarea (c. 260–c. 340) confirms some portions of the story. There was a Catherine of Alexandria, exceptionally well-educated for a woman of her day and devoted to the faith so unpopular with official Rome. Her punishment was not death, says Eusebius, but "translation" —which could be interpreted as exile and might account for the story of miraculous transportation to the sacred mountain.

The symbol of the wheel gives St. Catherine patronage over wheelwrights and millers; her wisdom and piety place philosophers and preachers under her protection. She is the patroness of nuns, maidens, and women students; hers was one of the heavenly voices that Joan of Arc heard in the forests of Domrémy, bidding the Maid go forth to save France.

Saint Crispin's Day

October 25, feast day of the Roman missionary brothers Crispin and Crispinian, the patron saints of shoemakers and leather workers, martyred in Gaul about 286 A.D. From the 15th century on, the day was especially celebrated in England as the anniversary of the victory at Agincourt, France (1415).

Crispin and Crispinian had fled Rome in 284 A.D. to escape the persecutions of the Emperor Diocletian. Making their way to Suessiona, Gaul (now Soissons, France), they continued to preach the gospel and supported themselves by cobbling shoes. Their success in converting many of the townspeople roused the wrath of Maximianus, who held jurisdiction over Gaul under the Emperor Diocletian. For a time the saints were able to emerge unscathed from the ordeals they were forced to undergo, but finally, his patience at an end, Maximianus ordered their heads struck off.

Buried at Soissons, their remains were later divided and reinterred, some at Osnabrück by Charlemagne (c. 742–814), some in the chapel of St. Lawrence in Rome. Their festival was observed for many centuries throughout Europe, but especially in the country of their martyrdom, with religious processions followed by merrymaking, in which the shoemakers' guilds took a leading part.

The battle of Agincourt, fought in a driving rain that turned the narrow field into knee-deep mud, was one of the more memorable episodes of the Hundred Years War (1337–1453). Although outnumbering the English several times over, the heavily armored French troops found themselves unable to maneuver on the sticky terrain against the more lightly clad archers and foot soldiers from across the Channel. They suffered enormous casualties, while British losses were almost negligible.

The victorious army had been led by King Henry V (1387–1422), and English pride in his triumph on that October day is echoed in the words Shakespeare puts into the ruler's mouth in *King Henry V*:

> "This day is called—the feast of Crispian . . .
>   And gentlemen in England, now a-bed,
>   Shall think they were accurs'd they were not here
>   And hold their manhoods cheap, whiles any speaks
>   That fought with us upon St. Crispin's day."

Saint Elmo's Fire

Brush discharges of electricity seen during severe storms as blue or bluish-white lights at the tip of masts and bowsprits of vessels at sea and on church steeples or other tall spires and prominences on land.

Saint Elmo, the patron saint of sailors—the name was originally Erasmus colloquialized to Sant' Ermo and thence to Elmo—was a bishop in the southern Italian province of Campania and was martyred during the Christian persecutions under the Emperor Diocletian (3rd–4th centuries A.D.). Naples is the principal city in Campania, and it was the sailors of that port who first came to look upon Elmo as their special protector. As they clung to the wet rigging of some storm-battered ship, they took heart from the eerie lights flickering around them as assurance that the good saint was watching over them and would bring them safely to shore.

In the 13th century, Portuguese sailors gave the phenomenon a different name. Having adopted Blessed Peter Gonzalez as their patron, they called the flashes "Saint Peter's lights." Today, however, the name in general use is once more St. Elmo's fire.

Saint Ignatius' Bean

The seed of *Strychnos ignatii,* a woody vine native to the Philippines, which in 1818 was found to yield the alkaloid poison strychnine.

The *Strychnos* genus, to which St. Ignatius' bean belongs, comprises some 220 species of trees, shrubs, and vines found throughout the tropical world. Strychnine is obtained from the bark and seed coats of various species, and its properties, both curative and lethal, have long been known. Small doses act as a tonic and stimulant; large amounts cause death through convulsions or by paralysis of the respiratory center of the brain.

The origin of the "bean's" name is obscure. The catalog of saints lists seven called Ignatius, one of whom,

Portuguese-born and surnamed Azevedo (1528–1570), spent several years on a mission to the Jesuit settlement in Brazil. Perhaps the appellation is derived from his activities there.

Saint-John's-Wort

A perennial, herbaceous plant growing wild throughout the United States and bearing yellow flowers edged with black spots.

There are at least 19 adjectival names for this showy bloom, one of some 300 species of Hypericaceae, including shrubby, bushy, creeping, straggling, and great. The Great St.-John's-wort, when cultivated, earns its title by attaining a height of 6 feet and sporting enormous five-petaled bright yellow flowers.

Because of its tufted stamens the Great St.-John's-wort is sometimes called *Aaron's beard* (*which see*), a name also applied to a related species, the Star of Jerusalem or creeping Rose of Sharon. A four-petaled species, pale yellow, is variously known as St.-Peter's-wort and St. Andrew's cross. In some areas, because of supposed healing properties, the plant is called tutsan, from the French *toute saine*.

Saint Martin's Summer

An unseasonably mild and pleasant spell of weather occurring in November (the kind called Indian summer if it comes in October).

St. Martin was a greatly beloved Bishop of Tours who lived in the 4th century and to whom a great many miracles were later credited. When he died, early in November, 401 A.D., in a little town some distance from his home city, the river vessel bearing his body is said to have floated up the Loire to Tours without benefit of oars or sails. All along the way the trees lining the banks burst into fragrant blossom, and unearthly music was heard until the ship slid gently to its landing.

Known as the soldier-saint because of his impressment at 15 into the Roman army, St. Martin left the service some years later to become a "soldier of Christ." The tale is told that while still a military man and riding fully armored through a town, he was accosted by a ragged beggar whom other townsfolk had jeered at or ignored. St. Martin, however, drew his sword, slashed his cloak in two, and gave half to the beggar to cover his nakedness. That night Jesus, wearing the same half-cloak, appeared to Martin in a dream and gave a heavenly blessing to the holy man.

Saint Patrick's Cabbage

(London pride). An ornamental member of the saxifrage family (*S. umbrosa*) with pale, crimson-spotted petals that show up well in rock gardens. The plant is native to the Iberian peninsula but also found in the mountains of west and southwest Ireland.

Saint Patrick's Day

March 17, anniversary of the death of Patrick, Archbishop of Armagh, the Apostle of Ireland (4th–5th centuries A.D.).

When St. Patrick was on a preaching mission in Ireland, he was taken prisoner by a pagan ruler and ordered to explain the Trinity. Bending down, he plucked a shamrock, now the Irish national emblem, and showing it to his captor, explained that just as the three leaflets are distinct yet united in a single plant, so the Trinity is the union of three distinct persons in One Deity.

Saint Swithin's Day

Feast day of the one-time Bishop of Winchester Cathedral, celebrated on July 15 and subject of the superstition that if it rains on Saint Swithin's Day it will rain for 40 days thereafter, while if it is clear, fair weather will follow.

Bishop of Winchester from 852 until his death on July 2, 862, Swithin (or Swithun) had been raised to that rank by the man he had once tutored, Athelwulf, King of the Saxons. Very little is known of the saint's life, but an 11th-century biography of some authority says that in addition to his many virtues he was a builder of bridges and churches.

When the bishop felt that death was approaching, he called the monks around him and exacted their promise to bury him not in the chancel but in the open churchyard where passersby might walk on his grave. Shortly after his death, he was canonized as a saint, and the monks deemed it unfitting that such a great and holy man should lie under the open sky.

His feast day, July 15, was designated as the time to remove his remains into the choir, but at the appointed hour a torrential rain storm broke, halting the proceedings for that day and 40 more. This was taken as a sign that the saint's wishes should prevail; as a compromise a chapel was built over the grave. A century or so later, when the church was restored under Ethelwold, the relics were transferred to the new basilica to the accompaniment, it is said, of many miracles.

An old verse runs:

> "St. Swithin's day if thou dost rain
> For forty days it will remain;
> St. Swithin's day if thou be fair
> For forty days 'twill rain na mair."

And there is an ancient saying that when it rains on St. Swithin's day the saint is christening his apples.

Saint Valentine's Day

The feast day, February 14, of two saints named Valentine, one a Roman priest, the other a bishop, both martyred by beheading on the same day in 269 A.D. during the reign of the emperor Marcus Aurelius Claudius and buried in separate graves some little distance apart on the Via Flaminia.

The linking of St. Valentine's feast day with the affairs of lovers seems to have been something of an accident. It was an ancient Roman custom on February 15, in honor of the goddess Juno Februato, for boys to draw out of an urn the names of girls, who then became their sweethearts for the year. After the advent of Christianity the idea grew of substituting the names of saints who would be considered patrons for the next twelve-month, and the day of drawing merged with the feast day of the martyred Valentines.

By Chaucer's time the legend was firm that birds began to pair on Saint Valentine's Day. In England and Scotland the drawing of lots by young men and women to determine their valentine was augmented, in a sort of mock betrothal, by an exchange of gifts. Later the exchange became one of ornate and fanciful written messages of affection, generally in verse.

Saint Vitus' Dance

(*chorea minor,* Sydenham's chorea; from Greek *choreia,* dance). A common term for the involuntary twitching and jerking of face, arm, leg, and other muscles, generally resulting from rheumatic infection, occurring mostly in children from 5 to 15, more often among girls than boys, and curable.

In Catholic hagiology, St. Vitus (or St. Guy) is one of the Fourteen Holy Helpers, a title that came to be applied in the Middle Ages to certain saints whose aid was invoked in particular circumstances: St. George by soldiers; St. Christopher by travelers; St. Catherine by philosophers, students and lawyers; and so on. When an epidemic of dancing mania swept Europe during the 14th, 15th, and 16th centuries, the victims made pilgrimages to the various chapels of St. Vitus, notably in Swabia, Germany, in the belief that prayers at his shrine would relieve their suffering. St. Vitus is also the patron saint of epileptics, perhaps because of a legend that credits him with having cured the son of the Emperor Diocletian of "mysterious seizures," although in fact Diocletian had no son.

The first accurate description of St. Vitus' dance was made by the English physician Thomas Sydenham (1624–1689). After his medical studies at Oxford had been interrupted by the civil war, during which he served four years under Oliver Cromwell, Sydenham made impressive contributions to medicine through his painstaking observations of the symptoms and course of diseases. He was the first to differentiate between scarlatina and measles. His great work, *Medical Observations,* was published in 1676.

Saint Wilfrid's Needle

A narrow aperture in the crypt of the cathedral at Ripon, Yorkshire, England, which is the subject of a local legend that a woman may be known to be chaste if she can pass through the opening.

The original cathedral, a basilica with columns and porches, built about 661 A.D. by Wilfrid, Archbishop of York (c. 634–709), no longer stands. Together with its monastery it was destroyed during the Danish invasion in the 9th century, and only the crypt was saved.

One of the few remaining examples of such Saxon architecture, St. Wilfrid's crypt has a central chamber for the display of relics and wall niches that once held lights.

The narrow passageway or needle is said to be "the old credence table with the back knocked out."

The cathedral that today houses St. Wilfrid's needle was begun by Roger, Archbishop of York, in 1154 and was subsequently added to during the next four centuries. In the south choir aisle is a slab to Robert Porteous (d. 1758), a cousin of George Washington.

Salome's Dance

The dance (of the seven veils) performed by Salome, daughter of Herodias, before the tetrarch Herod, who rewarded her with the head of John the Baptist.

The story is most fully told in Mark 6:17–28: Herod, although married to an Arabian princess, had taken his brother Philip's wife Herodias for his own. John the Baptist denounced the unholy alliance and thereby earned the hatred of Herodias. But Herod acknowledged John as a righteous man and, according to the Bible, "kept him safe."

On the tetrarch's birthday a great banquet was prepared for many guests, and Herodias' daughter, Salome, danced for them. So pleased was Herod that he vowed to grant her any request. Prompted by her revengeful mother, Salome asked for the head of John the Baptist. Reluctantly, but bound by his oath in the presence of guests, Herod ordered the execution. The guard "went and beheaded him in the prison and brought his head on a platter and gave it to the girl, and the girl gave it to her mother."

In the biblical story, Salome is not named but is referred to only as "the girl." She is said afterward to have married her uncle, Philip the Tetrarch. The name Salome is from the Hebrew *shalom*, meaning peace.

Oscar Wilde, in his play *Salome* (1893), rings a change on motive. Here the tetrarch is in love with his stepdaughter and bribes her to dance, against the wishes of the jealous Herodias. Salome is in love with the prophet John, who has harshly rebuked her; his head on a platter is *her* revenge.

Say's Law

That in a capitalist economy "the demand for products is equal to the sum of the products"; thus, that "a nation always has the means of buying all its produces"; and that while it is possible for overproduction of one or more commodities to occur, a general overproduction or "general glut" is impossible. The theory was put forward in the *Traité d'économie politique* (1803) by the French economist Jean Baptiste Say (1767–1832).

Scott's Bluff

An imposing rocky elevation rising 4,649 feet a few miles east of the Nebraska-Wyoming border, where the skeleton of fur trapper Hiram Scott was found in the spring of 1829. It was a landmark of the old Oregon Trail and is now part of the National Parks system.

An employee of the Rocky Mountain Fur Company in the 1820s, Hiram Scott had gone on a number of fur-trapping expeditions into the rich beaver country along the North Platte River. In 1828, while on one of his trips, he disappeared, and the following year his skeleton was found on the high bluff that today bears his name.

The details of Scott's misfortune vary considerably. It is generally agreed that he fell ill on the trail, that his fellow trappers found it impossible to carry him with them, and that they went off after promising to return with help. It also seems that the remains were found at a surprising distance from where Scott had reportedly been left—one account says 60 miles. But why the trappers abandoned their partner has never been explained.

Seward's Folly

The purchase of Alaska from Russia in 1867 by William Henry Seward (1801–1872), Secretary of State in the cabinets of Lincoln and Andrew Johnson.

The circumstances of the purchase of Russian America, as it was then called, are out of the ordinary. Hints that the Russians were willing to sell had been circulating as early as 1857. Two years later the Russian ambassador in Washington began negotiations, but with the outbreak of the American Civil War the matter was dropped. On a March evening in 1867, Baron Stoeckl called on Secretary of State Seward at the latter's home, with the declaration that his government was now ready to dispose of its holdings on the North American mainland.

Seward, long fired by ambitions for American Pacific expansion, was ready to buy. The price was settled with a minimum of haggling. The Russians wanted 10 million dollars, the American offered 5 million. They met at the 7 million mark, with 200,000 dollars thrown in for a long-established Russian fur-trading corporation, the Russian American Company. Seward immediately sent for State Department clerks, and by four o'clock in the morning the treaty had been drafted to the satisfaction of both parties.

The Senate, a bit stunned by this swift action, ratified the document on April 9, but the House stalled on voting the necessary appropriation. Nevertheless, the Russian government consenting, President Johnson took formal possession of the territory in a ceremony held at Sitka on October 18, 1867; and a reluctant House, faced with a *fait accompli,* voted on July 14, 1868, to pay its debt.

The practically single-handed acquisition for his country of some 600,000 square miles of wild and frozen land brought a shower of denunciations on the Secretary's head. Seward's folly was only one epithet. Seward's iceberg, Seward's icebox, Icebergia, and Walrussia were among others bestowed by irate politicians and journalists. Unperturbed, Seward stood his ground and dubbed the new territory Alaska, from the Aleut *alakshah* or *alayeksa,* a great country. History has not betrayed that name.

Shays's Rebellion

A revolt in 1786 against heavy taxes and general financial difficulties by the debt-ridden farmers and other poverty-stricken people of western Massachusetts; led by Daniel Shays (1747–1825), a former captain in the Revolutionary War.

The son of poor parents, Daniel Shays was born in Hopkinton, about 25 miles southwest of Boston. During the Revolutionary War Shays had advanced from lieutenant to captain, serving for a short time under General Lafayette, and had fought at Bunker Hill, Ticonderoga, and Saratoga. In 1780 he resigned from the army, and with his wife, Abigail, moved farther west to settle at Pelham in Hampshire County.

In 1783 the treaty with England brought peace to the colonies, but peace did not bring prosperity. Business was poor, taxes were exorbitant, and the paper currency in general circulation was vastly inflated, "not worth a Continental." Farmers, burdened with mortgages and suffering foreclosures and evictions, were especially hard hit.

In 1786 resentment boiled over. The Massachusetts legislature, controlled by wealthy and conservative men determined to protect their interests, had refused to issue any more paper money or make livestock, of which there was a surplus, legal tender. The angry farmers picked up their guns and marched. With Shays at their head they broke up a session of the State Supreme Court at Springfield and seized the town of Worcester. As the rebellion spread, armed bands shut down the courts in Northampton,

Barrington, and Concord. Demands were plainly put—paper money, a reduction in state debts, and a revision of the property qualifications for voting.

A small group of militia under General Shepard was sent out but had little effect in stopping the rebellion. Then in January, 1787, Governor Bowdoin ordered up a militia force of 4,400 under General Benjamin Lincoln; when Shays and 2,000 men tried to take the arsenal at Springfield, a pitched battle was fought, and he was defeated. He retreated into New Hampshire, where his camp was surrounded by Lincoln's troops. Shays and 150 of his men were captured; the rest escaped; and the rebellion was over. Fourteen of the leaders, including Shays, were tried and sentenced to death but were pardoned after the election of John Hancock as governor.

Snell's Law

The hypothesis that when a beam of light passes from one medium to another, the ratio of the sines of the angle of incidence and the angle of refraction is constant for the same two media; formulated by the Dutch astronomer and mathematician Willebrord Snell (1591–1626).

Solomon's Seal (David's harp)

A perennial herb of the lily-of-the-valley family (Liliaceae), having pale green or white bell-shaped flowers on an arching stem. It is so called because, when the old shoots die off each year, the scars that remain on the creeping rootstock are thought to resemble the markings on the magic ring or seal belonging to King Solomon (*see* King Solomon's Ring). The name also refers to a figure formed by two triangles interlocked to form a six-pointed star (Star of David), at one time used as an amulet to ward off fever.

Stephenson's Rocket

An early locomotive of an improved type, built by the English engineer George Stephenson (1781–1848), which in 1829 won a 500-pound prize offered by the Liverpool and Manchester railways.

The son of a colliery engine fireman, George Stephenson seemed destined to follow his father's calling. Born in the little town of Wylam near Newcastle-upon-Tyne, Stephenson at 17 could neither read nor write. But he had an active mind, and the mechanics of the pumping engine he tended at Killingworth mines whetted his curiosity. The first principles of a steam-driven stationary engine had already been established by Matthew Boulding (1729–1809) and James Watt (1736–1819), and to be able to study their inventions Stephenson put himself through night school.

In 1802 he took up watch and clock cleaning in his spare time and profited from his observations of their gears and mechanisms. The Welshman Richard Trevithick (1771–1833) had already built the first "road carriage" powered by steam. The possibilities in this use of steam power set Stephenson's imagination churning. By 1812 he had worked out certain changes in his pumping engine so that it could be used to haul tubs of coal from the loading areas to the mine-shaft exit, a job originally done by women and youngsters creeping on all fours and later by specially small-bred pit ponies. The following year he obtained permission to build an engine for transportation between the colliery and the port at the mouth of the Tyne.

A Stephenson locomotive pulled the first passenger train in the world in 1825, replacing the usual animal traction. Then in 1829 a competition was instituted, with a prize of 500 pounds, for an engine with the best combination of speed, power, and efficiency. Ten locomotives were entered; five dropped out on the morning the tests began. At the end of the seven-day trial Stephenson's Rocket was declared the winner; it had drawn three times its own weight at 12½ miles an hour and alternatively a carriage and passengers at almost twice that speed, at a minimum fuel cost. Cylinders set at an angle instead of vertically, and a boiler containing many small tubes that increased the heating surface, contributed to his spectacular win.

Over the years Stephenson continued to manufacture and improve upon his locomotives, although late in the 1840s, shortly before his death, he is said to have deplored the "railway mania." After his Rocket was displaced by more modern machinery, it was put in the science museum in South Kensington, London, where it may still be seen.

Stoddard's Way

A religious innovation instituted by the eminent Northampton, Massachusetts, preacher Solomon Stoddard (1643–1729), permitting all members of his congregation to partake of the sacrament of communion whether or not they had made a profession of faith, *i.e.,* undergone conversion.

Student's Distribution

A method of making allowance for error when taking samples for statistical purposes; introduced in 1908 by William Sealy Gosset (1876–1937), statistician for the large Irish brewery of Guinness. The method was so named because the company's rule, forbidding the publication of research by its staff members, was relaxed to permit Gosset to use the pen name A. Student.

Sutter's Gold

The ore deposits, discovered in 1848 in a mill race near what is now Sacramento owned by Captain John Augustus Sutter (1803–1880), which set off the great California gold rush of 1849.

Sutter (the name was originally Suter or Souter) had come to California by a roundabout route. Born of Swiss parents in the little town of Kandern in southwest Germany, he had seen a year's service as a member of the Swiss guard in the French campaign against Spain and clerked for a time first for a cloth merchant, then for a grocer. In 1826 he married Anna Dubelt and later started a cloth and yarn business, which was bankrupt by 1834. Reluctantly leaving his wife and four children (they rejoined him in 1849), he set out for America, where he hoped to found a Swiss colony.

He made his way to St. Charles, Missouri, and went on to explore the lands to the west. But his boat was wrecked in the Missouri River, and he lost everything. For a while he was a fur trader at Santa Fe. Then, having heard glowing tales of California, he decided to try his luck there. Traveling north and west, he passed through what is now Oregon to Fort Vancouver. It being too late in the year to risk the journey south through the mountain regions, he boarded a trading vessel, which took him on a five-month trip to the Sandwich Islands. From there he went to Sitka, Alaska, then turned south, and finally on July 2, 1839, arrived at San Francisco, called Yerba Buena at the time and part of Mexican territory. Here he chartered several launches for himself and the Kanakas he had brought with him from the Sandwich Islands, and the party began a tour of exploration up the Sacramento River. At the juncture with the Rio de los Americanos he dropped anchor on August 12, liked the place, and decided to stay.

The next years were occupied with building up his settlement, which he named New Helvetia (Sacramento). Granted 49,000 acres of land by the Mexican government, he expanded his first small adobe hut into the imposing structure known as Sutter's Fort and became a Mexican citizen and an official. In addition to the fort there soon sprang up a sawmill, a tannery, a blacksmith shop, and numerous other undertakings, while an active farming community flourished in the rich valley. Then in 1846 a revolt of California settlers against Mexico (the Bear Flag revolt) ended in the acquisition of the area by the United States.

The following spring Sutter decided he needed another sawmill and sent his partner, James W. Marshall (1810–1885), to look for a suitable location. A good spot was found at Coloma, about 40 miles east of the Fort, and by January, 1848, lumber cutting had begun. Then it was found that the tailrace was too shallow, and some time was spent in diverting the river to deepen the bed. Marshall went to inspect progress every day, and on January 24 he noticed some yellow grains gleaming from crevices in the exposed rocks. Collecting half an ounce or more, he hurried back to the Fort and behind closed doors disclosed his find to Sutter.

Sutter tried hard to keep the discovery a secret, but it soon leaked out. The rush was on. People abandoned whatever they were doing to go gold hunting. As word spread eastward the frantic race to California began, and by 1852 some 100,000 had crossed the country, with more coming by way of Panama and around Cape Horn.

Sutter himself was ruined. His property was overrun with squatters. A dispute that went all the way to the Supreme Court found the title to most of his lands invalid, and he was forced into bankruptcy. For a number of years he was granted a yearly pension of 250 dollars, but Congress turned a deaf ear to repeated petitions for larger reimbursement. On the evening of June 18, 1880, the day Congress once more adjourned without recognizing his claim, Sutter died.

Marshall fared no better. His claims were overrun too,

and his sawmill failed. By the time he died in 1885, a state grant of 9,600 dollars awarded him for his discoveries had been spent in further explorations for gold that proved fruitless.

Thor's Hammer

A huge iron, stub-handled sledge belonging to the Scandinavian god Thor, able to shatter anything it was hurled against and return to its owner's hand.

In Scandinavian myth Thor was the god of thunder, war, and agriculture, the son of Odin, king of the gods, and second to him in power.

Thor's wife, Sif, had wonderfully long hair that shone like gold and fell in shining waves to her feet. One day Loki, the god of fire and mischief, came upon Sif sleeping and cut off all her hair. When she awoke she was horrified, and Thor was enraged. He seized Loki and choked him until the god promised to go to the dwarfs in their underground workshops and have them make a new head of hair out of gold, which would grow like real hair on Sif's head.

The dwarfs quickly made a lifelike braid of fine gold wire. They also gave Loki two other gifts, Gungnir, a spear that would always find its mark, and a ship, Skidbladnir, that could be folded up small enough to fit into a pouch, but when unfolded could hold all the gods of Asgard.

On leaving the cave Loki ran into the dwarf Brock, to whom he showed his treasures. "Did my brother Sindri make them?" asked Brock. "If not, they can't be so wonderful." Loki flared up and offered to bet his head that Sindri could make nothing more marvelous. "Done!" said Brock.

Back into the mountain they went and explained the wager to Sindri. The dwarf took a pigskin and laid it on the fire, then handed Brock a pair of bellows. "Blow," he said, "and keep on blowing until I come back." Then he went out.

Meanwhile Loki had turned himself into a gadfly, and after buzzing about lit on Brock's hand and stung him. Brock howled with pain but kept up his blowing. In a little while Sindri came back and took out of the fire a live hog of radiant gold. He then put a lump of gold on the fire and went out again, leaving the same instructions as before. This time Loki-the-fly bit Brock on the neck until the blood came, but although the dwarf roared enough to shake the mountain he did not stop blowing. When Sindri came back he took a fine gold ring from the fire, laid a great lump of iron in its place and went out once again. As Brock pumped away at the bellows, the fly fastened just below his eyebrow and stung until the blood gushed down. The dwarf lifted his hand to wipe his smarting eye; at that moment the fire died down, Loki flew away with a mocking laugh, and Sindri rushed in.

"What have you done?" he shouted at his poor brother, as he drew out a huge hammer with a short, stubby handle. "Well," he went on, after looking it over, "perhaps it will do anyway, at least well enough to win you Loki's ugly head. Take the gifts and be off, both of you."

So Loki and Brock set off for Asgard, Loki in high spirits, for he could see nothing in a pig, a ring and a spoiled hammer to match his own gifts. Indeed, Thor was delighted with the crown of hair, which immediately grew upon Sif's head as if real. Odin was pleased with the spear, and Frey, the god of peace and fertility, with the remarkable ship. Loki was sure his head was safe.

Then Brock stepped forward. The ring, Draupnir, he gave to Odin, explaining that every ninth night, eight other rings as bright and golden would drop from it. "Why, this is better than the spear," exclaimed Odin. The gleaming pig, Goldbristle, went to Frey; this was a magic animal that could run on air and water and light up the darkest night, and Frey liked it better than the ship. Finally Brock handed the hammer, Miölnir, to Thor, apologizing for the short handle. But Thor was more than satisfied with his new weapon, for with it he would be invincible against the Frost Giants, the Trolls, and all the other enemies of Asgard.

Loki was now in deep trouble; he had lost his bet and his head was forfeit. But the master of trickery still had a trick or two. "You may have my head," he told Brock, "but not an inch of my neck. That wasn't in the bargain." And all the gods agreed that it was not. Thus cheated out of his wager, Brock took his awl and a stout thread, and sewed Loki's mischievous mouth shut—for a little while.

Tourette's Disease

A childhood psychosis marked by compulsive twitching and the urge, known as coprolalia, to scream out obscenities. It was first described in 1884 by the French neurologist Georges Gilles de Tourette (1857–1904).

Trendelenburg's Sign

A failure of those leg muscles connected with the pelvis to contract sufficiently to maintain balance when the subject stands on one leg, so that he falls toward the unsupported side. The symptom was described by the German surgeon Friedrich Trendelenburg (1844–1925) and recognized as evidence of hip disease in children. The "sign" has been observed where there is malformation of the head and neck of the femur, a congenital dislocation of the hip, or poliomyelitis.

Madame Tussaud's Waxworks Museum

An exhibit of lifelike wax models of the world famous and infamous, brought from France to England in 1802 by

Mme. Marie Tussaud (1760–1850) and now housed in a large red-brick building on Marylebone Road, London.

When Mme. Tussaud was still little Marie Grosholtz in Berne, Switzerland, she took great delight in watching her maternal uncle at his wax portrait modeling. Christopher Curtius was a physician by profession and at first had used his skill with wax to reproduce parts of the human body for study. He soon found the modeling of miniature portraits more congenial and eventually gave up practicing medicine altogether. Invited to Paris in 1762 by the Prince di Conti, Curtius took his sister and two-year-old Marie with him and settled down to the work he loved. About 1776 he began to produce life-sized models; shortly thereafter he opened a museum of these portraits at the Palais Royal. He followed this with a larger exhibit on the Boulevard du Temple, to which a few years later he added a *Caverne des Grands Voleurs*, forerunner to the famous Chamber of Horrors. Voltaire sat for Curtius in 1778 and Benjamin Franklin in 1783, the latter taking a number of miniatures back to America with him.

Marie became a skillful assistant to her uncle and in 1780 was asked to come to Versailles by King Louis XVI's sister, Madame Elizabeth, who wanted to learn the art of modeling. The two young women became fast friends, and Marie spent the next nine years at court.

Two days before the Bastille fell on July 14, 1789, she was called back to Paris by an alarmed Uncle Christopher. Her friendship with the royal family brought her under the suspicion of the Committee of Public Safety, and she spent some time in prison, where she met Mme. Josephine de Beauharnais, through whom Mme. Tussaud later came to do a portrait model of Napoleon Bonaparte. She was finally released, but as a price for her freedom she was made to preserve the likenesses of the victims of the Revolution. The features of Louis XVI, Marie Antoinette, Danton,

Robespierre, Hébert, the Princess de Lamballe, and dozens of others were recorded by her in wax, with casts, as she wrote afterwards, often taken from heads freshly severed by the guillotine.

Dr. Curtius died in 1795 and in October of that year Marie married François Tussaud, some seven years her junior, to whom she bore two sons. The marriage seems not to have been a happy one. When Marie transported her uncle's Paris Exhibition to England in 1802 she took her two little boys along but left her husband behind.

Established in London, she alternated her very popular showings at the Lyceum Theater with travels around the country, while continuing to add to her collection of figures. In March, 1835, she settled into permanent quarters on Baker Street where, according to her great-grandson and biographer John T. Tussaud, one of her first visitors was the Duke of Wellington. Attached to the museum was a house full of curios and mementos, and there she lived until her death on April 15, 1850.

Her sons and their descendants continued to operate the museum, which was moved to its present location on Marylebone Road in 1884. There is scarcely a figure of note that cannot be found there, while in the Chamber of Horrors, Jack the Ripper, Bluebeard, and other unsavory characters still go about their gory business.

There is a story told by Katherine Clemens, a niece of Mark Twain's, of a time when the author visited the wax-works. He had stood for some minutes admiring a particularly impressive group when he felt a sudden sharp pain in his side. Turning, he confronted an astonished English lady, her furled parasol still aimed spearlike at him. "Oh lor', it's alive!" she gasped, backed off and fled.

Ulloa's Ring

The fogbow, or white rainbow, faintly blue on the inner rim, faintly red on the outer, with a colorless band between; the very small size of the fog droplets preventing the diffraction that produces an ordinary rainbow. It was so named for the Spanish naval officer and scientist, Antonio de Ulloa (1716–1795), who on an expedition to South America in 1734 also discovered *platina* (the Spanish diminutive of *plata,* silver).

Venus'-Flytrap

(*Dioneae muscipula*). A small, white-flowered carnivorous or insectivorous plant of the sundew family (Droceraceae), found only in the sandy swamps of North and South Carolina.

Carnivorous plants grow in sandy, wet soil which is generally nitrogen poor; the insects, larvae, and other small life forms they trap and digest supply the necessary protein lacking in their environment.

The Venus'-flytrap operates in a rather special manner. The two halves of its leaves, edged with a dozen or so spiky projections, are set at an angle along the midvein. Reddish sap glands on the leaf surface provide the lure, and three little bristles trigger a mechanism that snaps the leaf halves shut over an intruder. The spikes rimming the leaf interlock like fingers, and digestive juices pour from the surface. In about ten days the body is dissolved, the leaves unlock, and the plant is ready for its next meal.

This particular species was first discovered in 1760 by the then governor of North Carolina, Arthur Dobbs, who named it the Fly Trap Sensitive.

Venus'-Looking-Glass

An informal name for plants in the bluebell family (Specularia), bearing blue or purple blossoms. There are four species native to America of which the bellflower or campanula is one. In southern Europe the plant grows in fields like a weed but is often put into cultivated gardens because of its startlingly beautiful purple flowers.

Vincent's Angina

(Vincent's infection). A slightly contagious, ulcerous condition of the mucous membranes of the mouth and throat (angina comes from the Latin for quinsy), caused by a bacterium and first observed by the French physician Henri Vincent (1862–1950).

Vincent's Gingivitis

An ulceration of the gums, so named when found to be caused by the same bacterium as that causing angina; also called trench mouth because of the high incidence of the disease among soldiers of World War I, induced by poor food, lack of sleep, and nervous tension.

Volta's Pile

The first electric battery, based on the discovery by the Italian physicist Alessandro Volta (1745–1827) that electricity could be generated when plates of different metals were brought into contact in an acid, alkaline, or salt solution. This effect was described by him in 1800 in a letter to Sir Joseph Banks, president of the Royal Society, London. The pile consisted of pairs of zinc and silver or copper disks, each pair in the same order, separated by thin sheets of flannel or paper soaked in brine. When the bottom disk (silver or copper) was connected to the top disk (zinc) by a wire, an electric current was produced.

Wallace's Line

An imaginary line through the Malay Archipelago between Borneo and Celebes, running roughly from southwest to northeast, which divides the islands into a western group with flora and fauna resembling those of India and the Orient, and an eastern group where the animal and vegetable life approximates that of Australia. It was drawn by the English naturalist, Alfred Russel Wallace (1823–1913), in the course of an exploratory journey through the archipelago, 1854 to 1862.

It was his observation of the sharp divergence of species that led Wallace quite independently to a theory of natural selection surprisingly close to Darwin's. On a trip through the Malay islands Wallace had fallen ill with fever, and while recuperating on the island of Ternate in February, 1858, he had sketched out his ideas "On the Tendency of Varieties to Depart Indefinitely from the Original Type." He sent it to Darwin, who recognized it as identical with a theory he had formulated some 16 years earlier after his own voyage of exploration on the *Beagle* (*see* Darwin's Finches).

More concerned about a useful contribution to science than in securing a first for himself, Darwin proposed that Wallace should make his theory public immediately. On the intervention of a mutual friend, however, the English geologist Charles Lyell (1797–1875), it was agreed that the theory should be brought out as the work of both men. Accordingly a joint paper was presented to the Linnaean Society on July 1, 1858, where it was received rather casually.

But after Darwin's *Origin of Species* was published the following year, and the full impact of the theory began to be felt in the scientific world, Wallace found himself in growing disagreement on a crucial point. Darwin had admitted of no exceptions in his evolutionary schema. Wallace held that man's spiritual essence set him apart, that the development of his mental powers had not depended on natural selection alone. As time went on Wallace became increasingly interested in such phenomena as clairvoyance and animal magnetism, and in 1875 he published *Miracles and Modern Spiritualism,* setting forth what he took to be experimental evidence for his beliefs.

Weigert's Stain

A purple dye (hematoxylin) made from the heart of the logwood tree and used in 1882 in the microscopic examination of degenerated spinal cord and brain tissue by the German pathologist Carl Weigert (1845–1904), who exploited the fact that the stain leaves healthy tissue clear and takes hold only where degeneration has set in.

Bishop Wilkins' Real Character

A system of writing, invented by the English Bishop of Chester, John Wilkins (1614–1672), in which the characters or symbols represent not sounds or letters but ideas or groups of ideas.

Puritan clergyman, brother-in-law of Oliver Cromwell, mathematician, and popularizer of science, John Wilkins was the leading spirit of that group of brilliant young scientists calling themselves the Philosophical College, organized in 1644 and which became the Royal Society in 1662. The Society was much influenced by the writings of Sir Francis Bacon (1561–1626), including his ideas on the philosophy of language. Bacon held that it should be possible to construct a language and a form of writing made up of "real characters," nonverbal symbols in the manner of Chinese ideograms, which could express things and notions without the use of words so as to be intelligible in any language. Shortly after its founding, the Society commissioned some of its members to examine the possibilities of such a universal real character, and Wilkins' *Essay Towards a Real Character and a Philosophical Language* was one of the results.

Utilizing Aristotle's notion of classification by categories, as Peter Roget was to do some two centuries later (*see* Roget's Thesaurus), Wilkins grouped all words expressing either things or ideas under broad headings according to kindred conceptions. Each heading was divided into genera, each genus subdivided by differences into species, and words within species were arranged in pairs of opposites. To each idea or "quality" expressed by the single words, Wilkins assigned a certain mark—a stroke verticle, horizontal, or aslant, a circle or semicircle in varying positions. Complete ideas could then be represented by assembling these marks in various combinations to form written "characters." Once the symbols were mastered, the ideas they represented could be comprehended regardless of the reader's native tongue.

Wilkins also proposed a spoken language on a similar basis. Here each genus received a syllable; differences were indicated by selected consonants; species by vowels supplemented with diphthongs. For students and would-be users of the language, a philosophical grammar, again based on Bacon's suggestions, was furnished.

The *Essay* was published by the Royal Society in 1668 (although the fuller treatise remained unfinished at Wilkins' death) and was received with lively interest. A former Curator of Experiments for the Society, Robert Hooke (*see* Hooke's Law), thought so much of the "real character" that he used it to write out the details of "the general ground of my Invention of *Pocket Watches*." The passage, in Wilkins' characters, appears as a postscript to Hooke's *A Description of Helioscopes,* published in 1676; it was decoded in 1936 by E. N. da C. Andrade, Professor of Physics, University of London.

Unfortunately, the character and the language were too complicated to become anything more than an ingenious exercise, and both eventually slipped into obscurity.

Wilson's Fourteen Points

A set of proposals put forward by President Woodrow Wilson (1856–1924) in an address to a joint session of Congress on January 8, 1918, which were to serve as a basis for settling World War I and establishing an international organization for a permanent peace.

Wilson first publicly voiced a proposal for a postwar federation of nations, with the United States participating, in May, 1916. Keenly aware of the underlying economic and political currents, Wilson saw a world league as the only hope for peace. In January, 1917, he spoke of it again, this time to the United States Senate and, in addition, offered a sketch of what he considered the war's end should bring—a "peace without victory," a peace not of indemnities or annexations nor any realigned balance of power, but a "community of power," a "peace among equals."

America's entry into the war that April, and the months of fighting that followed, did not change his views. In January, 1918, he presented to Congress and the world his comprehensive plan for putting an end to conflict by sensibly and intelligently wiping out the causes of conflict. He saw fourteen steps to this goal:

1. Open covenants, openly arrived at.
2. Absolute freedom of the seas outside territorial waters, in peace or war, unless abrogated by international action.
3. Removal of all economic barriers between nations, as far as possible.
4. Guarantees for reduction of armaments to the lowest point consistent with domestic safety.
5. Free and impartial adjustment of colonial claims, with

the interests of local populations to have equal weight with the interests of claiming governments.

6. Evacuation of Russia's territory, and opportunity for independent development under institutions of her own choosing.
7. Belgium to be evacuated and restored to full sovereignty.
8. All French territory to be freed, invaded portions to be restored, and Alsace-Lorraine returned.
9. Italy's frontiers to be readjusted along clearly recognizable lines of nationalities.
10. Peoples of Austria-Hungary to be given the freest opportunity for autonomous development.
11. Rumania, Serbia, and Montenegro to be evacuated; relations among the Balkan states to be settled by friendly counsel; political and economic independence to be guaranteed.
12. Turkish portions of the Ottoman Empire to be assured sovereignty; other nationalities under Turkish rule to be guaranteed autonomous development; permanent free passage of the Dardanelles to be internationally guaranteed.
13. An independent Polish state to be established, with access to the sea.
14. A general association of nations to be formed, which would afford mutual guarantees of political independence and territorial integrity to great and small states alike.

At the Paris peace conference in December, 1918, Wilson gained acceptance of the idea of a League of Nations, but concessions insisted on by various national interests left most of his other points badly shredded. In the summer of 1919 he returned home to face a hostile Congress and a

Foreign Relations Committee that refused to ratify the Versailles Treaty without drastic amendments.

To plead his case before the bar of his countrymen, and against doctor's orders, Wilson began a speaking tour of the United States, an enterprise abruptly ended at Wichita, Kansas, by a paralytic stroke. The remainder of his term of office was spent in the sickroom, from which he emerged briefly in the spring of 1920 to veto a makeshift Congressional resolution putting a technical end to the war. Not until President Harding had been in office almost a year was the Treaty finally accepted, and then only after insertion of a clause effectively preventing United States participation in the League of Nations.

Wood's Halfpence

Copper halfpennies in the amount of 108,000 pounds, intended for distribution in Ireland in 1724. The coinage contract was let to William Wood at an exorbitant profit to be divided between Wood and the Duchess of Kendal, a mistress of King George I of England.

Ehrengarde Melusina, longtime mistress of Prince George Louis of Hanover, had followed him from Germany when he assumed the English throne in 1714, and soon after became Duchess of Munster and Kendal. As the King's favorite she wielded a large influence, which she turned to good account by selling patent rights, titles, and public offices. In 1722 she was approached by William Wood, an impoverished iron merchant of Wolverhampton, who offered her 10,000 pounds to secure for him a patent to coin some 108,000 pounds worth of copper halfpennies for use in Ireland, which he claimed was suffering from a shortage of small coins. The venture would yield him a fine profit, since the metal, a copper alloy, cost only 60,000 pounds. Of the 38,000 pounds remaining after the Duchess had taken her cut, one-fifth would pay for striking the coins, one-seventh was required for patent fees, and the rest would be Wood's.

The proposal was made without prior consultation with either the Lord Lieutenant or the Parliament of Ireland. That country at the time was a complete English dependency. When the news that Ireland was to be flooded with a debased currency was received, the Irish Parliament and Privy Council dispatched a bitter protest to His Majesty.

The protest might have been lost except for Jonathan Swift, then Dean of Saint Patrick's Cathedral in Dublin. Seizing the opportunity, he wrote a series of six fiery letters, signed M. B. Drapier, denouncing the scheme and calling for resistance to it.

The first of the Drapier letters addressed to "the tradesmen, shopkeepers and people of Ireland concerning Wood's brass halfpence" appeared in April, 1724. The others—to "Mr. Harding, printer," to "the nobility and gentry of Ireland," to "the whole people of Ireland," and so on— were published between August and December of that year. The term "brass halfpence" drew a defensive rejoinder in Harding's newspaper, which noted that according to Sir Isaac Newton an assay taken at the Tower showed Wood to have lived up to his contract. Swift's letter to Harding countered by asking what proof there was that the "Dozen or Two Half-Pence of good Metal" sent to the Tower fairly represented the whole of the proposed coinage.

The doubts implanted by "Drapier," coupled with Ireland's genuine sense of insult in the handling of the matter, had their effect. By the time the fourth letter was published, the British were offering 300 pounds for the discovery of the author; by the time the last one had begun to circulate, Prime Minister Robert Walpole decided he had better give in. In 1725 the patent was withdrawn, Wood was compensated with a pension of 3,000 pounds for the next 12 years, and the whole affair suppressed.

Zeno's Paradoxes

A series of puzzles about motion and multiplicity, posed by the Greek philosopher Zeno of Elea (c. 490 B.C.) as indirect support for the doctrines of his friend and teacher Parmenides (c. 515 B.C.), who held that reality is one, indivisible, immovable, and eternal.

In reply to the charge that Parmenides' theory of the oneness of reality contained inconsistencies, Zeno offered his paradoxes to show that the assumption of manyness, many things in time and space, was even more inconsistent. Nothing Zeno wrote has survived, but eight of his paradoxes, intended to discredit ideas of plurality and motion, have come down through the writings of Aristotle and Simplicius. The three most widely cited paradoxes are the following:

1. Achilles sees a tortoise in the distance moving slowly ahead and sets out to catch up with it. But when he reaches the place A, where the tortoise was when first seen, the tortoise will have moved beyond that spot to B. When Achilles reaches B, the tortoise will have gone on to C. Therefore, however many times this process is repeated, the tortoise will always be that much ahead of Achilles, and he can never catch up.

2. Consider an arrow in flight. At each instant of flight, the arrow occupies a space equal to itself. But anything occupying a space equal to itself is at rest. Therefore the arrow is at rest.

3. Motion can never occur, because to reach a certain place one must first go half the distance; but to go half the distance, one must first go a quarter of the distance; and

to go a quarter of the distance one must first go one-eighth
—and so on.

Zorn's Lemma

One of a family of principles widely used in mathematical proofs and first proposed in 1935 by Max Zorn as
a convenient alternative to the famous axiom of choice (a
lemma being a proposition proved not for its own sake but
because it is useful in obtaining other results).

One of the chief features of the New Mathematics is its
emphasis on the theory of sets. Like geometry and other
branches of mathematics, set theory can be developed as a
system of theorems deduced from axioms. In the usual pres-
entation one of these axioms is the so-called axiom of
choice, which may be stated as follows: If S is a collection
of nonempty sets, no two or more of which have any element in common, then there exists a set C that consists of
one and only one element from each set in S.

Although the axiom of choice has been shown to be
consistent with the other axioms of set theory, it has never
seemed to mathematicians to possess the same degree of
obviousness. Despite its widespread use (in a bewildering
variety of equivalent forms, including Zorn's lemma), it is
still looked upon with reservations by mathematicians.

Index

Aaron's Beard, 1
Aaron's Breastplate, 1
Aaron's Rod, 1
Abraham's Bosom, 2
Achilles' Heel, 3
Adam's Ale, 4
Adam's Apple, 4
Adam's Needle, 5
Adam's Peak, 5
Adam's Rib, 6
Addison's Disease, 6
Apollo's Chariot, 7
Archimedes' Principle, 8
Ariadne's Thread, 9
Aristotle's Lantern, 12
Dr. Arnold's Rugby, 13
Avogadro's Hypothesis, 13
Avogadro's Number, 13

Babbage's Analytical Engine, 14
Bacon's Rebellion, 15
Balaam's Ass, 17
Bekhterev's Nystagmus, 18
Belshazzar's Feast, 19
Belzoni's Tomb, 20
Bluebeard's Wives, 21
Boyle's Law, 22
Boyle's 30 Acres, 24
Broca's Area, 25
Buridan's Ass, 25

Caesar's Wife, 27
Castle's Intrinsic Factor, 28
Cleopatra's Needles, 29

Cleopatra's War Trumpet, 31
Colter's Hell, 31
Coogan's Bluff, 32
Coxey's Army, 34
Cú Chulainn's Fort, 36
Custer's Last Stand, 37

d'Alembert's Dream, 39
Darwin's Bulldog, 41
Darwin's Finches, 43
Dido's Lament, 44
Diogenes' Lantern, 46
Dorr's Rebellion, 47
Down's Syndrome, 49
Dr. Eliot's Five-Foot Shelf, 49

Eratosthenes' Sieve, 51

Fermat's Last Theorem, 52
Fingal's Cave, 53
Ford's Peace Ship, 55
Ford's Theatre, 57
Foucault's Pendulum, 59
Fox's "Martyrs," 59
Fulton's Folly, 60

Godey's Lady's Book, 61
Goldbach's Conjecture(s), 63
Graves's Disease, 65
Gresham's Law, 65
Grimm's Law, 66
Gull's Disease, 67

Halley's Comet, 67
Hansen's Disease, 70

Harper's Ferry, 70
Hercules' Club, 72
Hercules' Labors, 72
Hobson's Choice, 76
Hodgkin's Disease, 77
Hofmann's Violets, 77
Hooke's Law, 79
Hudson's Bay, 80
Huntington's Chorea, 81
Huxley's Layer, 82

Ixion's Wheel, 82

Jablochkoff's Candles, 83
Jacob's Coat, 84
Jacob's Ladder, 84
Jacob's Pillow, 84
Jacob's Staff, 85
Jacob's Stone, 86
Jacob's Well, 86
Jacobs' Cavern, 86
Jacobson's Organ, 87
Jamie Keddie's Ring, 87
Jenkins' Ear (War of), 87
Jephthah's Daughter, 89
Job's Comforters, 89
Job's Tears, 91
Jonson's Learnéd Sock, 91
Joseph's Coat, 92

Kepler's Dream, 92
King Alfred's Cakes, 95
King Solomon's Ring, 96

Leeuwenhoek's Little Animals, 97
Lot's Wife, 98
Luther's 95 Theses, 99

MacFarlane's Lantern, 100
Macgillicuddy's Reeks, 101

Martha's Vineyard, 101
Mary's Little Lamb, 102
Maxwell's Demon, 103
McGuffey's Readers, 105
Mendeléyev's Table, 107
Mill's Canons, 107
Mohs's Scale, 109
Morgan's Raiders, 110
Morton's Fork, 112
Mother Carey's Chickens, 113

Napier's Bones, 114
Nat Turner's Rebellion, 114
Newton's Fits, 116
Noah's Ark, 117
Norman's Woe, 118

Ockham's Razor, 118
Olbers' Paradox, 119
Mrs. O'Leary's Cow, 120
Orion's Belt, 121
Orion's Hound, 122

Pandora's Box, 122
Parkinson's Disease, 123
Pascal's Amulet, 124
Paul Revere's Ride, 125
Peck's Bad Boy, 126
Penn's Woods, 127
Peter's Pence, 127
Pick's Pike, 128
Pike's Peak, 130
Plato's Cave, 131
Playfair's Axiom, 132
Poisson's Ratio, 133
Poor Richard's Almanack, 133
Potiphar's Wife, 134
Put's Hill, 135

Queen Anne's Bounty, 136
Queen Anne's Free Gift, 137

Queen Anne's Lace, 137
Queen Mary's Thistle, 138

Rama's Bridge, 138
Raynaud's Disease, 139
Ringer's Solution, 139
Robert's Rules of Order, 139
Robin Hood's Barn, 140
Roget's Thesaurus, 141
Roosevelt's Rough Riders, 142
Russell's Paradox, 144

Saint Agnes' Eve, 145
Saint Andrew's Cross, 145
Saint Anthony's Cross, 145
Saint Anthony's Fire, 145
Saint Catherine's Wheel, 146
Saint Crispin's Day, 147
Saint Elmo's Fire, 148
Saint Ignatius' Bean, 149
Saint-John's-Wort, 150
Saint Martin's Summer, 150
Saint Patrick's Cabbage, 151
Saint Patrick's Day, 151
Saint Swithin's Day, 152
Saint Valentine's Day, 153
Saint Vitus' Dance, 153
Saint Wilfrid's Needle, 154
Salome's Dance, 155
Say's Law, 156
Scott's Bluff, 156
Seward's Folly, 157

Shays's Rebellion, 158
Snell's Law, 159
Solomon's Seal, 159
Stephenson's Rocket, 160
Stoddard's Way, 161
Student's Distribution, 161
Sutter's Gold, 161

Thor's Hammer, 164
Tourette's Disease, 166
Trendelenburg's Sign, 166
Madame Tussaud's Waxworks
   Museum, 166

Ulloa's Ring, 169

Venus'-Flytrap, 169
Venus'-Looking-glass, 169
Vincent's Angina, 170
Vincent's Gingivitis, 170
Volta's Pile, 170

Wallace's Line, 171
Weigert's Stain, 172
Bishop Wilkins' Real Character,
   172
Wilson's Fourteen Points, 174
Wood's Halfpence, 176

Zeno's Paradoxes, 178
Zorn's Lemma, 179